THE

MYSTERIES AND MISERIES

OF

New York:

A STORY OF REAL LIFE,

By NED BUNTLINE

~~~~~~~~

PART IV.

NEW YORK:

EDWARD Z. C. JUDSON.

——

1848.

PREFACE.

WE have purposely permitted a considerable space to intervene between the publication of this and our last number, because we wished to watch the effect of that number, so as to temper the tone of this; for we have two aims in this work. One is, to do all the good we can with it; the other is, to make it as popular as possible, with the moral and respectable portion of the people, they being the only class for whose opinions we have any regard, and from whose praise we hope to gain a lasting reputation.

The tone of the following pages is formed from our observations since the issue of No. 3. That the work is popular with the reading community, we are forced to believe from the necessity of having to print *five large editions*, with a call already for a *sixth*.

In our last No. we named the location of several large gambling "hells," which are publicly kept open in this city. We did so, because we did not intend that those whose *duty* it is to enforce the laws of this State, should have any excuse for not performing their *duty*. The "hells" which we named are still in successful operation; they are crowded nightly by the young men of our city, clerks and students (and many a grey-headed man is there too), who go there to cope with the studied and professional gambler—the *shark* of immorality, who lives upon the verdant victims who crowd around him. Since the issue of our last No. one *clerk* in this city has proved a defaulter to the amount of *only* thirty thousand dollars! How much of this did the gamblers get? They or their unfortunate victim alone can tell. This one instance *proves* that our fictions are supported and surrounded by tragical *facts;* that we indeed are painting pictures of real life. And yet some persons, with a mawkish, mock sensibility, would condemn our pictures as "horrible and unreal."

The city papers of April 12th, after enumerating sundry police cases of theft, &c., contain the account of a man, who was *only* sixty-five years of age, committing a rape upon a poor girl of *eleven*, and then closing his career by suicide. In the Tribune of March 25th, we find this case:

"EXTREME DESTITUTION OF A CHILD.—H. Burnham, a boy about nine years old, was found in the street, by officer Rohenates, and covered with rags and filth. The child said he had no parents, his mother being dead about six months, since which time he existed on charity, begging for victuals from door to door, and at night crawled into a grocery charcoal box or some such place to sleep. He was sent to the Commissioner of the Alms-House to be taken care of."

In the same paper, a few days previous, we find another:

"DESTITUTION.—Policeman Van Tassel, while taking his rounds last night, found a female named Catharine Murray lying in one of the streets of the Second Ward, almost frozen to death."

These are not solitary and extraordinary instances; were we to go to the records, we could find many more.

Do we give scenes descriptive of more horror and guilt than the first named case, or of greater misery than the two last? Some who think we are describing New York as more impure than it really is, had better read the following report from *one* of the several prisons in this city:

"CITY PRISON STATISTICS.—Deputy Keeper Linden has politely favored us with the following statistics:

"Received into prison during the week ending March 4—White men, 93; colored men, 9; white women, 45; colored women 2. Total, 149. Sent to Blackwell's Island—White men, 19; colored men, 5; white women, 12. Total, 36."

Pretty well for one week, eh?

And yet there are more than one thousand *criminals* nightly and daily permitted to openly break a law of the land passed for their punishment and suppression. And these wretches are nightly dragging into their nets hundreds upon hundreds of the young men of the city, not only robbing them of gold, but of their decency and morality, making thieves of them, encouraging clerks to rob their employers; enticing the married man from his family, robbing his children of their bread, and his wife of her rights.

Why is this permitted? Are those men whose duty it is to crush the gambling hells of New York, all *cowards?* Or why do they dare to look the people, their *employers*, in their faces, when they know that they daily and hourly neglect their duty, which justifies us in pronouncing them *perjurers!* Hard words, but *true!*

Whose *duty* is it, to put in force the law to suppress gambling in this State and city? Who are those, who, when put in office, are *sworn* to do this and all other duties appertaining to that office?

In our last number, as a *trial*, we named the locations of *four* "hells" kept open every night. We sent marked copies of that work gratis to several Aldermen; a copy was sent to the Mayor,* twenty-five copies were sent gratis to the Police. And yet not one of these gambling houses has been disturbed—not one of these law-breakers has been even frowned at by the law-protectors.

While honest men and women are starving, while poverty and misery are all around us, money is plenty in these gilded "hells," and thousands of dollars are nightly exchanged in them. We have struck a harder blow against the gamblers, than we have against the *other* thieves in town, because we think them the most dangerous. We can trace the causes of the ruin of more young men to the gambling table, than to any other source in this city. Many a merchant has had good reason to curse the clan that has made a thief of a clerk in whom he placed confidence. The few burglars and pickpockets who are about,

---

* Since the preparation of this No. our city election has resulted in giving to us a new Mayor, and a new City Council. We have good reason to hope from the reputation which the present Mayor enjoys among the people, as a lover of good order, temperance, and strict morality, that he will take some steps to rid his city of the *pests* which we have named and pointed out. It will be an act that will reflect honor upon his administration, and be an infinite credit to the city. Even in New Orleans, the gamblers find far more trouble and prosecution than they do here. Let them either be *licensed* at once, and made to pay the city a part of their stealings, as they are obliged to do in Mexico; or else let them be broken up. The city is in debt—the citizens are grumbling at a heavy taxation, and yet there is not a night passing that could not be made worth *one hundred thousand dollars* to the city, if each gambling house was entered, and its *professors* arrested and *fined*, to the extent of the law which is provided for their punishment.

at great peril and risk manage now and then to steal a few dollars; a cloudy night, or careless watch, sometimes favors them. But it matters not to the genteel robber of the "faro banks," or "roulette table," whether it be rain or shine, he can steal with open impunity; though *he* breaks the *law*, it matters not, for 'he knows it will not be *enforced* upon him. He is a *gentlemanly* robber.

Once more we refer to this subject, and for the last time that we shall do so in this mild way. We shall again see that a copy of this work, calling upon the officers of the law to do their duty, is sent to them; and if, after this, they neglect their duty, we will publish the names of those who not only act so *cowardly*, but fail to fulfil their *oaths* of office, and we will do it in good company too, with the villains whom they will not, or dare not prosecute.

We are aware that, in taking this stand, we place our weak and single arm against the whole *army* of gamblers in this city; we have received many hints of their not very friendly feelings to us, and acknowledge the receipt of numerous threatening communications, but we do not care a groat for the whole crowd. If we are not supported by the men whose *sworn* duty it is to suppress them, we know that we will be by the moral and respectable portion of the community. Our own conscience supports us, and though we have to stand *alone* in this warfare, we will not shrink from it, while life is left in our body.

A marked copy of this work will be sent gratis to every Alderman in the city, and also to the City Counsellor, and if we can find them, to the members of the Grand Jury. The Appendix of our third No. and the tenth chapter of the same work, contain the locations of the " hells " which are named.

We simply named those *few*, for a commencement; there are plenty of others which are not kept at all secretly, all of which must and shall be stopped, or the people shall know who those are that *dare* to neglect the duty for which they are hired and *paid!*

PART FOURTH.

CHAPTER I.

WHEN Angelina, our poor sewing-girl, fled from the house of Mrs. Windeman, frightened by the reappearance of Gus Livingston, she knew not where to go. Her first thought was to return to the panel-crib of her new-found cousin, but two thoughts at once arose to prevent her from going there. The first, was her knowledge of the character of that house; the second, a fear that Lize had something to do with the appearance of Livingston; that she, led away by some new and tempting inducement, had betrayed her.

This was a cruelly unjust thought, but Angelina did not pause to consider how directly contrary it would have been to all the former conduct of the poor panel-girl, whose character, with all its faults and vices, certainly did not possess the stain of faithlessness. What she was, she knew and felt, but too well; what she had been, she still remembered; and she was too open-hearted to pretend to be what she was not. In fact, she was of that character which we rarely, yet sometimes, *do* meet—one who was *honest* in her open acknowledgment of all her faults. Not that she would openly acknowledge her guilt to all, for she could either be silent or give vent to " virtuous indignation" before a magistrate, or she could be whatever she wished to the verdant stranger whom she wanted to inveigle into her crib. A talented woman was she in her way.

But to return to Angelina. When she left her boarding-house, she hurried on, trembling at the sound of every footstep behind her, directing her course towards the northern part of the city. She almost ran, while she was in the crowded and busy thoroughfares of the city—but she became very weary in a little while, for she was weak in body and sick at heart. As night came on, she had reached a quiet street in the upper portion of the town, one of those few streets not used by the omnibus lines, and traversed by few vehicles except an occasional private carriage belonging to one of the wealthy dwellers in that neighborhood.

Her steps were now very slow—she felt faint at heart and a dizziness seemed to come over her brain, and to throw a mist before her eyes. The twilight began to deepen—still she wandered on, not knowing where to go or what to do.

At last she felt that she could go no further. She saw a young lady advancing, wrapped in a warm cloak, her hands folded in a large muff, and she determined for the first time in her life to *beg*. The young lady was attended by a well-dressed young man, and both of them appeared to be of the wealthy class, by the rich and fashionable appearance of their garments.

Angelina timidly looked the young lady in the face as she came near, and with a voice trembling from emotion as well as fear and cold, said:

"Please, Miss, aid a poor helpless girl to get a place to lodge in to-night. I will work, indeed I will."

The young lady paused a moment, for Angelina stood right before her, then turning up a little pug nose, which was slightly blued by the cold, replied:

"I haint got no change! have you any, brother Alfred Eustace?"

"Yes, but not for the likes of her!" responded the young man, with a careless glance at the trembling girl, "there are lots of places where she can get lodgings free, and make money by it too, down town! Come along, Sis, she's not fit for you to speak to!"

And young Alfred Eustace Fitzroy Fitz Lawrence hurried his sister away, after making his last coarse and unfeeling insinuation, leaving the wretched Angelina standing alone upon the icy pavement.

It was now dark. "Oh God of mercy, let me die and go where my mother is!" murmured the poor girl.

She staggered to a door step close to her, and seating herself upon it, burst into tears. But she tried to hush her sobs as she heard foot-steps approaching, and almost held her breath, for her first attempt at begging had so chilled her, that she did not feel like speaking to another passer-by. But the person who now approached didn't intend to pass, he turned to the very steps where she sat, and was passing up them, when her half-stifled sobs, which she could not suppress, fell on his ear.

He stopped, and descending to the corner where she was seated, close up against the iron rail, asked in a voice which sounded rather gruff, but still not unkind:

"Hallo! what's this—what's this? Who are you on my door step at this time o' night?"

"Forgive me, Sir, I'll go, but I was so tired!" murmured the poor girl.

"Where to—where do you live?" asked the gentleman, now looking more closely at her.

Her only reply was a fresh burst of tears. She could hold in no longer. That question told her how utterly homeless and desolate she was.

"Poor girl—poor girl! Now don't cry, but tell me what's the matter!"

She would have spoken if she could, but her sobs choked her utterance.

"Poor creetur!" murmured the gentleman in a pitying tone, and he passed his hand over his own eyes, as if to wipe away a sympathetic moisture there.

The kindness of his tone seemed to assure poor Angelina that she need not fear an insult from him, and when he again asked her where she lived, she replied, that she had no home now.

"No home, child? Now be a good girl and don't tell me stories. I can't abide 'em. Where is your father and mother?"

"Dead—both dead!" sobbed the girl.

"No brothers nor sisters?"

"No—none! I am all alone!" responded the poor girl.

"Why how have you lived? Where did you live until now?"

"I lived with my poor mother till she was—till she died, and then I went with a woman who said she was my cousin, but I saw a man who frightened me and I ran away!"

"A man that frightened you? Did he mean you harm?" inquired the gentleman still more kindly.

"Yes, Sir, he had insulted me before, and I was *so* afraid of him!"

"And you have no home now?"

"No, Sir!"

"Poor creetur! I must do something for you, I must! Let me see; if I give you money, do you know where to find lodgings?"

"No, Sir, indeed I do not. I'm afraid to go down town—there are so many men in the street who will insult a poor girl like me!"

"Right—you *are* right, my girl. I believe you are good. I can't see you well here, but you weep and tell a very straight story. You don't walk the streets at night?"

"Oh, no, Sir! God save me from that!"

"Amen, my good girl! I believe I can trust you. I'll give you a home for to-night at any rate. You shall have some warm supper, and tell me all your story, and then you shall sleep with Jenny my house-maid!"

"God will bless you, Sir!" murmured the poor girl, gratefully. She obeyed him, and followed him to the basement door of the building before which they had stood. He rang the bell, and in a moment the door was opened by a neat, tidy-looking girl, who held a light in her hand.

The maid looked surprised as she saw that her master was followed by a young girl, and as the latter rather held back, the gentleman very kindly said,

"Come in, my dear, come in out of the cold!"

Then turning to the maid who had opened the door, he said:

"Jenny, here's a poor girl who has no home. Give her some supper and treat her kindly!"

"Yes, Sir," said the maid, dropping a low curtsy, but looking very suspiciously at the poor creature "who had no home."

They now entered the little sitting room in the basement, where a very cheerful fire was blazing.

A young man was seated before this, with a book in his hand, apparently very intently engaged in its perusal, but he arose as the party entered.

"Ah! Francis," said the old gentleman, "reading away, eh? good boy—*very* good boy!"

The maid now assisted the old gentleman off with his hat and overcoat, while the young man took them from her, and placed a chair for his master.

"Never mind the chair for me, Francis, I shall go up to my parlor," said he, "but here's a poor girl whom you and Jenny must be very kind to! Hurry and get her some supper!"

"Yes, Sir," said Jenny,—"but, Sir, have you had suppe" yet?"

"No—really no! Well, I had forgot all about that. Nevei mind; give her some as soon as you can. Poor creetur, how thin she looks! She must have had a deal of trouble!"

Then, when he had made her take her bonnet and shawl off, he continued, speaking, as if to himself:

"Poor creetur! how pale—she would be pretty if it wasn't for that!"

Then he turned to Francis and said,

"Come up stairs with me, Francis, I want you a little while!"

"Yes, Sir," said Frank, laying down his book.

Before the old gentleman had reached the door-way, he was stopped by the little housemaid, who whispered:

"Is *she* to stay here all night?"

"Yes, Jenny, of course she is! She has nowhere else to go!"

"Then where is she to sleep?" asked Jenny quickly.

"Why with you of course. You have a large double bed!"

The little servant maid seemed struck dumb with surprise at this announcement.

"Why, Sir," she gasped, "you've picked her up in the *street*. How can I tell what she is? I don't know what I've done, Mr. Precise, to be treated so! I'm sure she's some bad girl, and if she sleeps in my bed, I won't, that's all!"

Jenny's voice had risen from the low whisper to a pretty loud key before she closed this last speech, and poor Angelina could not help hearing it.

"I will sleep anywhere—here on the carpet, or on the settee!" said she timidly, "I don't wish to offend that young lady."

"Young *lady* indeed!" cried Mr. Precise angrily—"why she's not half as good as you are, poor girl, for she has no feelin' for a sufferin' fellow creetur. You shall have her bed, and if she don't choose to share it with you, she may find a place some-where else !"

"Then I will, so I will !" replied the maid indignantly, looking rather wickedly at Frank, "and what's more, Mr. Precise, I'll not stay in a house where I'm treated so, so I won't. I'll not be turned out of my bed for every strumpet you choose to bring home with you !"

Poor Angelina heard this cruel term, and again bursting into tears, said to Mr. Precise—

"I'm not what she calls me, Sir, indeed I'm not. No, Sir, if I would be bad like many other girls, I would find plenty of homes in this city—I would not have been a homeless wanderer at this hour !"

"That's true, my good girl ! I believe you ! your very tears tell your tale !" replied Mr. Precise, kindly ; then turning to Jenny, he added :

"You may choose your lot now, Jenny ; either act like a Christian, or leave my house !"

Finding that her angry and indignant mood could have no effect, Jenny now altered her tone, and said :

"If you say she is good, Sir, I suppose she must be—but I don't like this takin' up with everybody as comes along, so I don't !"

"I don't care what you like, Jenny ; I like to do my duty as a man and a Christian ; and now hurry and get supper for us all ! The poor girl must be mainly hungry ; any one can see it by her looks ! Don't cry any more, my dear, I'll be a friend—yes a *father* to you ! After you've had your supper, you shall tell me all your story, and I'll see what I can do for you ! Poor creetur, I'm sure she's had a hard time on't ! Come along, Francis—we must attend to business to-night. I've been talking about my new plan for a 'Home for the Poor' and I mean to draw up a plan for a company, for I'm too poor to do it all by myself !"

"If you please, sir," said Frank, recollecting that he had an engagement at Jack Circle's, "if you please, sir, my poor mo-ther is very low ; I'd like to go and see her for a couple of hours. I'll be up bright and early to attend to your business in the morning."

Mr. Precise paused a moment before he made a reply, for his

heart and head were both full of his new plan for doing good : but at the end of that thoughtful moment, he replied :

" You're a good boy, Francis, to *love* your mother. Go and see her. Here, take this" (handing him a ten dollar piece) "tell her to buy medicine with it, or anything to make her comfortable. She has a good son; tell her that I, Peter Precise, say so."

" Yes, sir," replied Frank, looking at the money as if he really felt ashamed to take it. Then he asked :

" May I go now, before tea ?"

" Yes, my boy, if you want to. Jenny, be careful and lock the street door behind him ; and I say, Frank !"

" Sir ?"

" Be home early, my boy !"

" Oh, yes, sir, you may depend upon me !" cried the young rascal ; and as if perfectly satisfied that he could depend upon Master Francis, the good old gentleman ascended to his parlor, bearing a new pleasure in his bosom—the thought that he had given a home to a desolate one, that he had closed the day with a truly Christian and charitable act.

How many of our readers who are wealthy, or, at least, *have to spare*, beyond the means necessary for their comfortable sustenance, can say this for one hundredth part of their ending days ?

When Mr. Precise had left the basement, Frank busied himself in putting on his outer garments to prepare for his walk, at the same time glancing often at Angelina, who had seated herself sadly before the fire, as if he wished to make out what kind of a character she could be. He had seen so few poor girls in the city like her, who wore the appearance of virtue, that he could not comprehend her.

Jenny, meantime, without speaking to, or hardly glancing at the poor friendless girl, busied herself in preparing for supper, until Frank told her he was ready for going out.

She then took the light to see him to the door and close it.

" This *is* somethin' new in our master !" said she, as soon as Frank and herself got into the entry or hall which led to the outer door, she having closed the inner one behind her.

" New, but not strange ! just like him ! he *is* a warm-hearted old covey !" replied Frank.

" Well, I don't like it, so I don't ; and as to sleepin' with her, I *won't*, that's flat !" said Jenny.

" Well, what'll you do ?   Sit up and cry all night ?"

" No, I won't do that !"

" Well, what will you do ?"

" I'll—, I'll—, Francis, I'll—you know what I mean !"

" No, 't wont do now, Jenny. She'll blab to the old man. You must be careful now ; remember what Shakspeare says—"

" I don't care what Shakspeare says, Frank ; I don't want to sleep with that 'ere creetur as he's picked up in the streets. May be—she—she keeps boarders in her upper story !"

" What?   Ah, yes, I understand. You mean she may be flush with *creeping* ideas ?"

" Yes ; and I don't like to sleep with her !"

" Well, Jenny, my love, as Byron says, ' there *are* antipathies,' but I think you are safe ; the girl looks nice and clean ; you'd better run the risk !"

" Well, if *you* say so ; but Francis, dear, will you be home early ?"

" Yes, my dear, if you'll sit up for me !"

" To be sure I will ; but will you come *sober ?*

" Of course, my dear ; I was slightly elevated the last evening I was out, but I met some old friends, and the imbibatorial spirit overcame me a little !"

" Yes, and it was *so* lucky master didn't find it out !"

" So it was, my dear : good night !" and imprinting a hearty kiss upon the buxom maid's pouting lips, Frank made his exit.

CHAPTER II.

It was an hour later. Mr. Precise had finished his supper, Jenny had cleared away the table, and now the old gentleman sat before the comfortable fire in the back parlor, listening to the tale of Angelina.

He heard her in simple but touching language relate how she and her poor mother had striven and suffered since her father's death; how they had worked for their bare and scanty living; and he shuddered as her tale reminded him of poverty which he had already witnessed in one instance at least. And when she came to that part which told of the villany and persecutions of Livingston, the old gentleman *almost* swore, so angry was he at the thought that she, so young and helpless, should be pursued and insulted, simply because she was poor and beautiful.

But he calmed himself to listen to her continuation. When she told him about her mother and herself seeking a home in the "Brewery," he stopped her and asked her all about the place. Her replies satisfied him fully of her truth, and when she told him of the horrible murder of her mother, while her utterance was checked by her sobs, tears poured down his cheeks.

He did not check her, however, until she had told all, and then he paused and sighed several times before he ventured to speak.

"Poor creetur!" said he at last. "You've had more trouble in your short life than I have *ever* seen, and I'm old enough to be your grandfather!"

Then he sat still, and looked at the fire very intently for nearly half an hour, without speaking. Then suddenly bringing his hand down upon his thigh with a heavy slap, which so frightened poor Angelina that she started from her chair, he said in a determined tone:

"Yes! I'll *do* it!"

Then while Angelina was wondering what he meant, he turned to her and said :

"My dear, wouldn't you like to live with me all your life, and be a daughter to me ?"

"I'm willing to work for you, sir, if you'll give me employ- ment," replied Angelina. "I can sew very well, and I think I could do housework, only I've been very weak lately !"

"But I don't want you to work much. Only to sew a button on for me now and then. I've neither chick nor child in the whole world to love—no one to leave a dollar to—no one to leave my name with. If you'll live with me, and be a good girl, I'll be a father to you !"

The young girl did not reply. Tears stood in her large eyes; her lips trembled with emotion, but she could not speak.

Mr. Precise did not wait for her answer, however. He again brought his hand emphatically down upon his knee, and said :

"Yes, you shall be my own daughter. I'll educate you like a lady. You shall bear my name, and when I die, you shall have all I own !"

The door opened at this moment, and Jenny appeared, her face being very red, too, as she entered.

"Did you call me, sir ?" she asked, looking first at Angelina, and then at Mr. Precise.

"No, Jenny, I did not, nor do I want to be disturbed !" re- plied Mr. Precise, in a sharp tone.

"I only thought——I thought I heard you call !" said Jenny, turning very red, and darting a spiteful glance at the sewing- girl.

"Then you made a mistake. You may go to your work again !" said Mr. Precise, sternly.

The waiting-maid did not reply, but turned away with a scornful shake, which much agitated the voluminous skirts of her garments, and slamming the door behind her, left the apart- ment.

The reader will better understand the reason of this conduct, when informed that Jenny had spent the twenty minutes prior to her appearance, in listening at the key-hole of the back-parlor door.

After she left, Mr. Precise again spoke to Angelina.

"Would you not like this arrangement, my dear?"

Still she did not answer. "I *like* you!" he continued, but noticing a start and glance from her, he quickly added—"as a daughter!

"You've had a hard time of it, but you have withstood temptation, and been good and virtuous where hundreds would have fallen. You deserve a reward, and Providence seems to have thrown you in my way, purposely!"

The poor girl sighed, but yet did not speak. Mr. Precise grew impatient for an answer.

"Why don't you speak, my dear?" he cried—"don't be afraid of me!"

"I'm not afraid, sir," answered she, "but you are *too* kind. I am willing to work for you—I must work while I *live*, but that will not be *long*. I feel that I am going very fast. For more than a year I have been sinking!"

"No, no! don't say so. I'm sure you'll soon be well. You are a little pale and thin now, it's true, but you shall not suffer any more, and you'll live a long—long while yet!"

"No, sir, I think not. I feel as if my time had nearly come. But I don't wish to live—I'm so lonely!"

"No, no! don't say so, my poor girl!" cried Mr. Precise, much affected by the sad, yet resigned tone in which she spoke. "You shall not be so lonely again. *I'm* very lonely now—but we will be company for each other. I'll have teachers for you: you shall learn music and be a lady. I'll treat you just like a daughter!"

The young girl sighed again, and a few scattering tears stole out from her large blue eyes and ran hurriedly along her cheeks, which were not so pale as they had been. A red flush was gathering upon them, and also on her forehead. Yet her lips were growing more pale.

She made no answer to Mr. Precise, but he, noticing her heightened color, thought it was the warm flush of pleasure thrilling through her veins, at the thought that a better day was dawning upon her young life.

"How beautiful you look, my dear!" said he, "why I do declare your cheeks are as rosy as a Spitzenberg apple!

The young girl smiled sadly at this compliment from the *good*

25

old bachelor, and turned to brush away the tears which ran down her cheeks, but her heart was brimful of grief, and an occasional drop would run over in spite of her attempts to check it.

And yet her color grew brighter and brighter all the time. She pressed her thin, pale hand to her brow, and her breathing seemed to be difficult. Alas! that temporary flush of beautiful red, was not significant of pleasure or joy, newly budding in her poor broken heart. Like the rosy fleece of sun-gilded clouds, which often bespread the sky, just before the breaking out of a fearful storm—that sky which seamen term "mackerel"—this flush upon her cheek gave token of a fever already coursing through her veins.

Mr. Precise saw her little hand pressed against her forehead, and asked in a kind tone:

" Does your head ache, my dear ?"

" Oh yes, sir, *very* much ! It is very hot !"

The old gentleman looked at her lips as she spoke, for he heard her voice tremble, and he noticed that they were very white, and quivered as she spoke.

" Poor girl, you are feverish ! You must go to bed ! You shall have a doctor !"

" Oh no, sir, I am not very sick ! don't go to any expense for me !" murmured the girl, who indeed felt sick.

" But I will !" said the old gentleman, feeling her pulse and at once detecting the fever—and he hurried to the bell and rang it.

The maid took her own time to answer it, for after waiting several minutes, Mr. Precise had taken hold of the bell-pull to ring it again, when Jenny made her appearance:

" Did you want me, sir ?"

" Yes, to be sure I did, you lazy huzzy ! Why don't you move when you hear me ring !"

" I *did* come, sir !" replied the maid spitefully, looking angrily at poor Angelina, as if to say, "this is all your fault—I'd like to scratch your eyes out."

" Then go for a doctor, and be quick about it !"

" What, sir, are *you* sick ?"

" No—confound it—hurry along, and don't stand there to ask questions !"

Jenny turned to go, but she had one more question to ask.

"What doctor shall I call, sir?"

"WATSON, to be sure! I never have any other inside of my doors, you know!"

"But, sir, what shall I tell him?—you are not sick!"

"Confound the girl, she'll drive me mad! Go and tell him I want him as soon as he can come! Now hurry!"

Having now no more questions to ask, Jenny retired, moving, however, very slowly.

Mr. Precise had heretofore been patient, but his red face grew much redder than usual, and following her to the door, he said angrily:

"Jenny, if you behave in this way, I'll discharge you in the morning!"

"Then you'll have to pay me my month's wages—for you hav'n't given me *warning!*"

"So I will—but I don't care, I'll not put up with your impudence!"

"It's all along of your bringin' that nasty little good for nothin' into the house!" replied the maid, putting her apron up to her eyes; "I never was treated so before, I wasn't, and it's too bad it is, after bein' so good to me as *you* have, and makin' me *love* you so!"

Jenny now began to sob very loudly, thinking that tears would subdue her master, if her angry tongue could not, but he was not in a humor which she could reach, for he slammed the door to, without replying again.

"Well, I *never!*" cried Jenny, ceasing her sobs as the door closed—"I do believe he's gone stark stavin' demented! I'll make *her* pay for this—I will! I'll get a doctor, and I'll take my own time a doing on it too! *She* sleep with me indeed! I reckon there's two to make a bargain about that! Why I'd rather sleep alone all my life—and that would be dreadful! Oh dear, I wish Francis was here! This last whim of my master's beats everythin' in Shakspeare all holler, so it does!"

While Jenny was thus indignantly soliloquizing, she was preparing to go after the doctor, which she did after a delay of full half an hour.

Meantime the fever was rapidly rising in the burning veins of poor Angelina, and though she did not murmur, or utter one word of complaint, her quivering limbs, throbbing pulse, and mildly flashing eyes, all told of the fearful progress of pain and disease.

Her frame, which had been so long supported by the unnatural excitement of grief and suffering, and by her stern resolve to work on and not to give up, had at last failed, and with it the very strength of her heart and soul too fled away.

Mr. Precise watched the poor sufferer, as she lay there upon his sofa, and often did he go to the door and look out, to see if the doctor was not coming. Frequently, too, he brought her water to cool her parched lips; and though she said nothing, he felt more than rewarded for his kindness by the grateful looks she returned, when her hot head sank back to the cushions, after partaking of the cooling draught.

The doctor came at last, and when he looked upon his patient he sighed, for he was a kind-hearted man.

"You should have sent for me before!" he said, in a low whisper, to Mr. Precise; "I'm afraid she will not have strength to bear the medicine necessary to break such a fever. She is very weak!"

"Poor thing! Do all you can for her!" said Mr. Precise, wiping away a couple of great tears which tickled his cheeks, as they ran down two ravines, leading to the corners of his mouth.

"Yes, yes. We must hope for the best, and do all we can. Have her at once undressed and put to bed in a cool room; I will make out a prescription!" replied the doctor, taking one of his cards out, and writing upon it.

Mr. Precise again called for Jenny, and she, who really had no wish to leave her place, and had many reasons for desiring to keep it, now obeyed him, and assisted in placing the poor girl in her bed. She also hurried to the nearest apothecary's for the medicine, and quite made Mr. Precise forget her former misconduct in her present officiousness.

Mr. Precise himself sat and watched by the side of the sufferer, preparing her medicine with his own hands, and really seeming to feel as much interest in her fate, as if she were indeed his daughter.

In finding such a friend for poor Angelina in this last deep trial, God had indeed proved that he cared for the fatherless !

CHAPTER III.

WE presume that you are curious, reader, to know the fate of the unfortunate sister of Charles Meadows.

We left her, just entering the room of Emma Wood, while Henry Whitmore, in a fearfully angry mood, was ascending the stairs.

When he reached the landing, Emma asked in a tone as careless as she could assume :

"Where is she? Has she not gone out ?"

"Curse me if I know !" replied the libertine. "She has hardly had a chance, for the door opening to the entry was not closed; we must have seen her if she had passed that way !"

"But where can she be? Didn't she go out by the back-door?" asked the woman, wishing, if possible, to keep him from the right track of his victim.

"No," replied he, "I tried that door, and found it locked on the inside. I believe she 's in the house yet, and if she is, by the Hand that made me, I 'll have her !"

Whitmore sternly looked Emma in the face as he said this, and while he noted how pale she turned, and that her eye avoided meeting his, his suspicions became aroused, and he cried in a stern and bitter tone :

"Emma, I'm not in a humor to be trifled with ! If you know where she is, you'd better give her up! I warn you now, for hell is in me to-night !"

For a moment the courtesan kept silent. Oh ! what a moment of agony was that for poor Isabella ! There she lay, within three steps, and heard the terrible threat, and she knew that one word from the lips of the woman, nay, one sign from her hand, would disclose her place of concealment, and then, what could she, a weak, terror-stricken, helpless girl, do against his inhuman force and strength !

And when the courtesan spoke, the wretched girl, for one moment, was thrown into the unutterable agony of believing herself betrayed, for the woman replied to Whitmore :

" I *do* know where she is ! You must think you *are* somebody, to scare *me* with your big words !"

" I don't want to scare you, Em !" replied the villain, lowering his tone a little, " but if you know where she is, just tell me !"

" Don't you wish I would ?" said the girl sarcastically.

" Yes, indeed I do. Come, Em, I'll give you an X."

" Not enough !" replied the girl carelessly.

" Then, I'll double it !"

" Not enough yet !"

" Why blast the thing, Em, you must think I'm made of gold !"

" No, I don't ! You're like Sam Selden, there's more brass in your composition than any other metal !"

" Well, Em, dropping all these compliments, what will you take to tell me ?"

Oh ! how poor Isabella trembled while she heard this conversation !

Emma Wood paused a moment after Whitmore's last question, and then said :

" A cool hundred !"

" Well, tell me ?"

" Hand over the tin !" replied the woman.

" I've given you nearly all I have with me. I'll let you have it to-morrow ! I've nothing but a twenty dollar bill."

" No—no ; to-morrow is a bad pay-day !" replied the girl.

" I'll give you my note !"

" I don't want your note—I'd make a pretty face trying to collect it, wouldn't I, if you chose to refuse payment. They'd ask whether it was for value received, I suppose !"

" Blast it, you seem to want to plague me to-night !" cried Whitmore angrily ; then, as he glanced at his hand, he saw a ring which Isabella had in an hour of confidence and fondness placed on his finger. It was a diamond, set in a very antique manner, and had been an heir-loom in her family—one, which she would never have parted with, except to an affianced husband. Glancing at this ring, Whitmore said:

"Here's security. There's a ring worth double the money. You may have that if you'll tell me!"

"Well, give it to me!" said Emma.

In a moment it was on her finger.

Isabella was about to spring from beneath the bed where she had crept, and had determined to leap from the window even at the risk of destruction, when Emma said to Whitmore:

"She is in the street somewhere! I saw her go out when you was talking to me in the back-parlor!"

"Curse you! is this your information!" cried Whitmore, almost bursting with anger.

"Yes. Ha! Ha! I've done you out of the ring, eh?" laughed the girl.

"Which way did she go?" shouted Whitmore.

"How could I tell? I saw her slip out of the entry, and I wasn't agoing to tell, for I do think it's a shame for you to hunt that poor girl about so, when there's plenty prettier ones and good enough for you too, that are ruined now!"

Whitmore paused a moment to think what plan to pursue. If, as Emma said, Isabella had escaped, he supposed that she would be able to reach her home before he could overtake her; and moreover, he knew that if she had once actually gained the street, it would be a difficult and dangerous business for him to try to bring her back when policemen and others were continually passing.

Isabella now began to breathe more freely, for she hoped that the courtesan would not betray her.

Whitmore again looked at Emma, and he still noticed that her eye was averted from his gaze, as it had been while she spoke. He felt sure that she had not told him the truth, but he determined to find it out if possible. Dissimulation was his plan.

"Well," said he, "if I *must* give up the chase, I suppose I must, but it is hard to lose twelve or fourteen hundred dollars for nothing on a poor chit of a girl like her!"

"It would have been harder for her to lose what all the gold in the world could not buy back to her—her virtue and purity!" said Emma, coldly.

"So it would, my fair philosopher, and we'll drop the subject!" said Harry carelessly, and then he added:

"I'll go home, I believe, or up to Carlton's! you're too cross for my company to-night!"

Thus saying, he turned away, passed down the stairs, and in a few moments Emma heard the street door slammed heavily after him.

She then went into her own room, where Isabella met her with tears of gratitude.

"Oh! God bless you!" she cried, kissing her fervently, "you have saved me from worse than death. Oh, that I had the means of repaying you!"

"You have repaid me!" replied Emma "one such pure kiss as that, one such prayer for God's blessing on my guilty head, is worth a thousand such acts!"

Who would have thought it! tears, great warm tears, came from that lost girl's large black eyes!

The well of human feeling was not quite dried up in her heart. Though steeped in guilt, though hardened in her very misery, she proved that there were yet fruitful spots in her heart; that there was at least one sunny spot in her character. And who will dare to say that such as she cannot be drawn from the sea of wretchedness where they have fallen? Who will say, pass them by and let them perish! Oh God! why should the cry of perishing thousands go up in this city, and no aid be extended to them!

Some will say, aid *is* offered; that charities are established, that we have our Magdalen Asylum, our Indigent Female Asylum, &c., &c., but let them see how difficult it is for those who need aid, to get admission to these places. Few are *requested* to enter; some, by working very hard, may obtain admission, at the expense of nature's choicest jewel, self-pride, or self-respect.

We have said before, in this work, and we say it again, that of the numerous systems for reformation adopted and used by the good and benevolent in this city, many do more harm than good; and others do far less than they should, because not properly directed—not conducted with a due regard to the natures of those whom they would reform. They have beautiful theories, but practice proves them to be worse than useless.

The nearest approach to a useful and proper means of aid and reformation to the guilty and wretched, which we can imagine, is that which Mr. Precise proposes, under the name of " A HOME FOR THE POOR," in the fifth chapter of Part II. of this work.

But to return to our story.   Emma Wood's heart was touched by the blessings and caresses of the poor girl whom she had tried to aid, and she determined as soon as possible to get her out of that house and its impure neighborhood.   Therefore she said to Isabella :

" You must not stay here ! he will be sure to come back and find you—you know your way home ?"

" Yes, but I feel *so* weak !" murmured the girl.

"Never mind, I'll go and get you a carriage !" said Emma ; " I'll not be gone a moment.   Lock the door inside, and when I come back I'll give three knocks, and you'll know it is me.   Ah ! what made you start so?"

" I thought I heard a noise outside of the door !" replied Isabella, trembling.

Emma stepped to the door, looked out in the entry, but saw no one.

" It was only your fancy !" said she, and then continued :

" I'll go and get you a carriage, and see you safe in, and then I shall feel contented."

" I feel afraid to stay here alone," sighed Isabella.

" Oh ! no one will come in.   I'll lock the street door behind me as I go out, and I'll not be gone more than a few minutes !"

" Well, go, I will try to be calm," murmured Isabella.   And yet when Emma left her, the poor girl turned still more pale, and trembled as she heard the sound of her steps dying away in the distance.

She locked the door inside, as she had been directed, however, and then knelt down by the bedside and prayed—prayed fervently to God to save and protect her in the peril which environed her.   Her heart was full of dread, yet ; she could not feel safe under that roof.

Only a few moments elapsed, when she heard quick steps ascending the stairs, and her heart for a moment almost stopped beating in her anxiety.   But she heard the signal, the three low taps upon the door, agreed upon to denote the return of Emma, and she hurried to the door to open it.

As she drew back the bolt, the door flew open, and she shrieked as she saw Harry Whitmore before her!

She would have fallen to the floor, but his arms clasped her, and he drew her form to his breast, now swelling with the pride of his villanous triumph.

"So, so, my fair lady! thought you was free, eh! You didn't know what a persevering lover you had! Ha! ha!"

She did not hear his taunts. She did not feel the burning and passionate kisses which he imprinted on her lips. She did not see the fiery glances which he bestowed on her form, beautiful even in its disordered dress, her face lovely in even its deathlike pallor.

"Fainted, eh? so much the better for me; I can manage her more easily!" he muttered, and then raising her from the floor, he bore her out, and closing the door behind her, hurried down stairs. He carried the still senseless girl into the front parlor, and closing the door which opened from that room into the entry, awaited the return of Emma Wood with the carriage.

He had but a moment to delay, for, as he closed the door, he heard the wheels of the approaching carriage dashing along the pavement.

In another minute the hack stopped at the door, Emma hurried out, and telling the driver that the lady would be out in a minute, passed by the door where Whitmore stood with the insensible girl in his arms, and hurried up stairs. The moment after, Whitmore stepped noiselessly out, and finding the hack door open, quickly lifted poor Isabella in, saying to the driver:

"It's all right, my man, go ahead!"

"Is this the sick lady, Sir?" asked the coachman.

"Yes—yes, drive on!" cried Whitmore impatiently, for he feared the return of Emma Wood to the door.

"Where to, Sir?" said the driver.

"To 100 Church Street!" replied Whitmore, "and be quick; she is very sick, I want her taken home!"

"What to old Ma'am Swett's?" asked the driver, as he closed the door.

"Yes, to be sure; be quick, and I'll give you a *ten spot!*"

"Oh, very well, Sir!" said the driver, making more haste, "if it is to be paid for, I'll do my work and ask no questions, but that's a funny place to take a sick young *lady* to, I think!"

He drove off, just as Emma, finding her room tenantless, came down stairs. She could not comprehend the reason of this, until she saw a white scarf which had been worn by Isabella, lying upon the door step, and then she thought that Isabella had gone into the carriage of her own accord, and hurried the driver off.

"I do think it was a little ungrateful of her to go off, and never say good bye!" she said, "but the poor thing was frightened out of her wits!"

Little did she dream that the wretched girl was again in the power of her infamous persecutor, and that he was bearing her away to a den of infamy, where no one would raise a hand to save her; where all were so low and vile, so guilty themselves, that they would only glory in aiding to make another as bad as they were.

This he knew well, and when he found that he could not complete his villany at Madame I.'s, he determined to take his victim to a place where he would be secure from interruption.

It was late, and his carriage drove along through silent streets, but it had not very far to go, ere the driver drew up before the house which he had named.

"Ring the bell and ask Madame S. to step here a moment. Tell her Harry Whitmore wants to see her!" said Whitmore to the driver, as the latter opened the carriage door.

"My fare first, if you please, Sir!" said the driver, who had evidently dealt with some of the fancy city bucks before.

"Certainly, and if you'll give me your word not to tell the woman that hired you, where you drove to, or that you saw *me* at all, I'll give you a *twenty!*"

"Done. I'll keep as mum as a mouse when the cat's about!"

Whitmore handed him the twenty dollar bill and the driver then rang the bell. In a few moments the door was opened, and in answer to Whitmore's message, a middle sized, dark-eyed, red-faced specimen of fallen *wom*anity made her appearance.

Whitmore whispered his wishes in her ear, and told him that his victim was there in his arms senseless.

"I've only one objection. All my rooms are occupied!" said she.

"Who has the third story, back room?" asked Whitmore.

"French Rose!" replied Madame S.

"She pays you ten dollars a week for it!"

"Yes!"

"I'll give you a hundred, if you'll let me have everything my own way!" said Whitmore.

"And let me keep the girl when you cast her off?" asked the woman, while her dark eyes flashed brighter than usual, at the prospect of gain.

"Yes, if you can. I don't want her long. I want to break that infernal pride of hers, and make her pay for the trouble she's given me!"

"Well, then, you may have that room, but the front garret would be more quiet. There are thick shutters on the side that fronts the street!"

"Well, well, anywhere, so that I can be quick. She acts as if she was coming to!" cried Harry.

"Then bring her in!" said the trafficker in the misery of her sex.

As Harry obeyed, and lifted the poor girl out of the carriage, the fresh air somewhat revived her, and opening her eyes, she saw the face of Whitmore.

She screamed faintly and struggled to get away, but he instantly put his hand over her mouth, and was hurrying in, when a lot of young fellows who were just going in turned and met him on the steps. They were evidently some of the b'hoys, and tolerably elevated.

"Ello!" cried one, "what's this ere chap a doin'?"

Seeing that they were not men with whom he was acquainted, Whitmore tried to push on, while Madame S. replied to the first speaker:

"It's only one of my girls drunk, and this gentleman is taking her in."

"Well then, let her slide!" said the b'hoy, "but I say, old 'oman, aren't you agoin' to stan' treat?"

"Oh! go away now, and don't make a fuss!"

"No, we don't, old lady, if yer don't stan' treat. We're the b'hoys, *we are, ourselves!*   We've brought a strange b'hoy here to see your house, and you've got to treat, bee the Laud—yer have !"

" Well—well, go in, and I'll treat if you'll keep quiet and don't kick up a row !" replied the landlady.

The carriage now drove off, and Whitmore having carried his victim up stairs, the landlady entered the well-furnished parlor with her forced guests.

Her dark eyes flashed angrily as she saw the b'hoys spout their tobacco-juice over her beautiful carpets, but she dared not say anything to offend them, else her looking-glasses and other furniture would have been sure to suffer *some.*

It was strange, but true, that though she cared little for the police, or any who had a legal right to enter her doors, and disturb her establishment, she scarcely dared to call her soul her own before the new-comers.

They ordered wine—she got it for them ; they kissed her girls, and cuffed them round to hear them squeal, yet no one thought of resisting their " innocent familiarities."

At last, when the wine was brought up and poured out, the one who hailed Whitmore on the steps, cried out :

" Are ye all loaded and primed, *gents ?*"

Each of the b'hoys replied, as they held a brimming glass aloft :

" We aint nuthin' else, Mose, *we* aint !"

" Then fire away !   *No,* hold on, till I interduce the strange b'hoy to the boss she !" cried the young man who seemed leader of the crowd, and who was known by the antique, but abbreviated cognomen, " Mose."

As he said this, he led out a short, dandified, grey-eyed, light-haired, brown-whiskered individual, and addressing himself to Madame S., said :

" Lookee yer, old 'oman ! this ere chap is one of the b'hoys, and he's from down east, he *is !* We've taken him in, and he's one of *us !* He *is* a little *dressy,* but that's nuthin'—he's a tailor, and carries his sign on his back !"

" What's his name ? I think I've seen him before !" said the landlady, fixing her dark eyes upon him.

" Oh ! well, *you* may call him Smith or Jones, jest as you like, but we calls him the Apostle, we does !"

"Why so? He don't look very like a preacher!"

"No," replied Mose. "Nor he don't look werry like a soger, but he *is*, and a *full* private at that. Why, he's one of the b'hoys, I tell yer, and nuthin' else! He's a traveller, been to *Holmes's Hole* and other sich places of worship. Here's to him—let's drhink!"

Mose set the example, and soon the bumpers had disappeared down sundry exceedingly capacious throats.

"Well, wots to pay? Wots the damage?" asked Mose.

"Let me see, three bottles champagne—nine dollars for the general run o' folks, but only *seven* for you!" replied the landlady, who began to hope that the b'hoys would for once pay up; but when Mose spoke again, her hope fell still-born.

"Don't yer wish you may get it?" he said, making the masonic sign with his thumb resting upon the end of his nose, and his four fingers performing sundry singular antics near the end of the nasal member.

"Yes, I do!" she replied spitefully.

"Then charge it to profit and loss. You'll rob Peter to pay Paul, you'll not lose by it!" replied Mose.

"I hopes you're not personal, Mister Mose!" said the down east b'hoy, turning rather red in the face.

"Well—don't know as I vos, but if yer think so, and want to make a muss about it, why jist say so! that's all!"

"No—I don't want to make no row!" replied the fellow, turning exceedingly pale, as he regarded the decidedly combative attitude of Mose, "only as you call me the 'Postle, I didn't know, Mose, but you meant suthing in that last speech!"

"Well, then, there wont be no row in this ere meetin'—but I say!" said Mose, again confronting the landlady, "d'ye know Jack Scott?"

"No, nor I don't want to!" replied Madame S., who was quite put out of sorts by such unprofitable customers.

"Well, you needn't be quite so crusty about it. Jack Scott and Bill Kirby are b'hoys, they are! Ned Forrest *is* some, but he aint a touch to Jack Scott when he wraps himself up in the star-spangled banner and goes for to die! three cheers for Jack Scott!"

Three hearty cheers were given, which Madame S. neither

joined in nor approved of, for she cried, as soon as her voice could be heard ;

"Don't make so much noise, for Heaven's sake, gentlemen ; you'll have the police in here—you'll ruin me !"

"It's cussed hard to spile a rotten egg !" cried Mose, "an' as to yer police, jist bring on a cord or two on 'em. We can lick the crowd, *we* can !"

No police came, and the b'hoys becoming tired of the fun there, proposed going to some other gilded hall of infamy to put the "she boss" through, as they had Mrs. S.

They therefore left her, and she was very well satisfied to get off from such a crowd with so little damage.

The moment after they had gone, Whitmore came down stairs, and handing Madame S. a key, said :

"You'll have to go and doctor that fool of a girl. I cannot get her out of her fainting fit. The moment she opens her eyes and sees me, she goes off again. I'll leave her till to-morrow evening, and so you attend to her and try to bring her to herself. Tell her not to be a fool. I have determined to make her mine, and mine she must be, willing or not !"

"I'll see what I can do with her, Harry !" said the landlady, taking the key from him, "but wont you take a glass of wine ?"

"No, I thank you," replied he, "I'm going round to Carlton's to win four or five hundred, and I want to keep my nerves steady. Wont you lend me fifty to begin with ?—I'll return it to-morrow !"

"Certainly !" replied the landlady, "you've first-rate security in the house !" and she laughed as she took the money from her purse and handed it to him.

CHAPTER IV.

WHITMORE hurried from Church street around to the hell of Carlton. It was quite a fashionable hour when he arrived. The guests of Mr. C. had supped and were already clustered before the other table, behind which Mr. Sam Selden sat, assisted by a genteel-looking grey-headed gentleman, who acted as banker in the absence of Mr. Carlton, who had other business to attend to just at that moment.

Whitmore first visited the side-board, and partook of some of Mr. Carlton's extra-fine brandy, in order to settle his nerves for the game. As he was pouring out the liquor, a tap upon his shoulder caused him to turn quickly around, and he saw standing before him, *Charles Meadows.*

The shock of seeing him was so sudden, and Meadows looked so pale, that Whitmore for a moment entirely lost his self-possession, and dropped his half filled glass to the floor, where it was shivered into atoms. But as he saw that a faint smile was forming on the countenance of Meadows, and that his face, though haggard and pale, did not wear the looks of anger, the self-convicted villain recovered himself enough to respond to the friendly salutation of the young clerk.

"Why, how pale you look! are you sick?" asked the latter of Whitmore, as he noticed his evident agitation.

"No—yes—that is, I'm not sick, but I'm not very well. I felt dizzy just now, and came to take some brandy to try and settle my nerves!" replied the villain.

"Well, I'll join you, I'm not well to-night, myse f," said Meadows.

"No," responded Whitmore, "you look badly—what is the matter?"

"Nothing, only I've rather over-worked myself lately!" replied the clerk, with a carelessness which completely re-assured Whitmore.

They both filled their glasses with brandy slightly diluted, and drank.

"Do you intend to play to-night?" asked Meadows.

"Yes, I believe I'll try my hand. I've a fifty to lose will you play?"

"No, I think not," replied Meadows, "I'm rather short just now—had to give my mother a hundred this evening, for rent!"

"Go me halves, with mine?"

"Thank you, Harry, but I'd rather look on and see you play. You always win!"

"Yes, generally in all kinds of games!" said Harry, with a smile, which would have seemed meaning to any one, except one so confiding as Meadows.

They turned to go to the faro-table, but just at that moment another person entered, whom they waited for. It was Gus. Livingston. He looked surprised to see Whitmore there, but calmly returned the salutation of both the young men.

"Why, where have you been, Harry? I've been looking everywhere for you. I just left the Count and a crowd at Jim Decatur's room, at the C——n, where they were having a quiet little private game of poker—I thought you'd be there!"

"No,—that's a small potatoe crowd!" replied Whitmore; "I've been spending a very agreeable evening in the company of ladies. I just left Charley's sister and mine; by the way, Charley, Miss Isabella is a very fine musician!"

"Yes, she has a very fine natural taste, and I've had the best masters for her!" replied the unsuspecting brother.

Livingston had exchanged glances with Whitmore, and thought by the look of the latter that he had triumphed. Filling a glass for himself from a decanter on the side-board, he said:

"I'll propose her health! Join me in it!"

"With all my heart!" said Whitmore, "may she be always as happy as she is now!"

"Ha! ha! she ought to be happy in having such a demnition fine fellow for a —————— brother!" said Livingston, in a singular tone.

Meadows did not notice the tone, but poured out another glass and drank it off. He was evidently bent upon trying to drown the memory of his guilt.   He did not even object to a third glass before they approached the faro-table.

When they took a stand in front of the dealer, Whitmore looked at Sam Selden, and cried:

"Here, Sam, let's have this fifty broken into five dollar checks. I'm going to win my night's expenses!"

Taking up the fifty dollar bill which the young man tossed over to him, Selden bowed very politely, and passed it to the banker, who soon handed out its equivalent pile of red checks.

"Ready for the deal!" said the handsome gambler, showing his white teeth, and smiling upon the betters.

"Don't *abbreviate*, Sam, just say ready for the *devil!*" cried Harry, placing five of his checks upon a card.

"Dem'd good, that, Harry!   More truth than poetry!" cried Gus. Livingston.

But their conversation was cut short as the deal commenced.

Whitmore has placed his money upon the Jack, and in a few moments it was drawn, and upon his side.

"The *knave* wins, sir," said the polite Selden, smiling maliciously as he emphasised the word.

"Ha! ha! he hit you there," cried Gus.

"Will you take up your bet, sir?" asked Selden of Whitmore.

"No, let it lay, the *knave* may win again!" said Harry.

The deal went on, and the knave not only won once, but four times in succession, leaving Whitmore the winner of four hundred dollars on that card.

"There, that'll do for to-night!" said Harry, when the deal was out, "just hand me over the change for those checks—I don't want any more just now!"

'Where'll we go?" asked Gus., as the three young men drew back from the crowd which fronted the faro-table.

"Anywhere, for fun!" said Harry. "I've no engagements this evening!"

"Morning, you mean.   It's after twelve!" said Meadows, looking at his watch.

"Well, it's no matter.   Let's go and have something to eat, Florence is open yet!" cried Harry.

"I'd rather drink!" said Meadows, "let's go upon a bender, I haven't been on one for some time now!"

"Agreed!" cried the other two, and by way of a foundation for future potations, they took another glass of Carlton's brandy.

"Well,—which way?" cried Meadows, whose spirits began to rise with the effects of the liquor.

"Wont you go to Jule's, and see the angel of darkness that fooled you so nicely—Kate Hall?" asked Whitmore.

"No, not there. I've had enough of her!" replied Meadows.

"Let's go to old Swett's!" cried Gus. Livingston.

"I'm agreed, anywhere!" cried Meadows.

"But *not* there!" said Whitmore, quickly. "I won't go to Swett's!"

"Why not?" asked both the others.

"Because I don't like her place—it's a low hole!" replied Whitmore.

"So much the better—we can kick up a spree there and nobody 'll know us!" said Meadows.

"Well, if you *will* have it so, go ahead!" said Whitmore, in a bitter tone, "but may-be you'll wish you hadn't gone!"

"What the devil sets you against her so!" asked Gus. Livingston with surprise.

"Oh nothing, go on, I'll follow!" cried Whitmore.

The three now started out, but at the front-doorway they were met by Carlton.

He smiled as he saw Meadows.

"You're the very man I was thinking of, Meadows!" said he, "and the one whom I wished most to see!"

"Ah, indeed! Well, sir, you *do* see me!" said Meadows, with difficulty repressing a shudder, as he gazed upon the man and remembered the dreadful scene of that morning.

"Yes, but I must see you alone!" replied the gambler, in a pleasant but decided tone.

"I'm just now engaged. You see I have company!" said Meadows.

"I can't help it, sir," replied Carlton, "business must take precedence of pleasure!"

"This is no business hour!" said Meadows sulkily.

"*Hours* were not specified in your *bond!*" said Carlton in a low whisper, bending his head close to Meadows's ear.

The young man turned ghastly pale, and rather groaned than spoke :

"What do you want with me?"

"Dismiss your companions, and come with me. You shall soon learn!" replied the gambler sternly. "Remember, sir, that you are mine now, body and soul!"

Poor Meadows felt that this, alas! was but too true, and turning to his comrades, said :

"I can't go with you, boys. Carlton and I have business together which I had forgotten. You must excuse me!"

"Certainly!" cried Whitmore, glad of any excuse which would break off this proposed visit to Church street.

"Well, did you ever!" said Gus. as Carlton went up stairs with Meadows. "Why Charley turned as pale as a ghost when Carlton whispered to him. He don't seem to dare to call his soul his own—what can 'cow' him down so, before Carlton?"

"I suppose he owes him money," said Whitmore. "Charley hasn't got hardened yet, enough to look a man boldly in the face whom he owes!"

"Poor fellow, he's too tender-hearted to belong to our set then!" said Gus. "Why if Jim Decatur and the Count and some of the rest of us didn't owe all the tailors and jewellers in town, we'd be miserable. Charley can't be aware of the exquisite pleasure one feels in damning a dun! But I forgot—where's his sister?"

"In bed I suppose!" said Whitmore, who seemed not to feel particularly communicative.

"Well, how did you get along after I left you?"

"Well enough!" said Whitmore, and then before the other could ask any more questions, he added :

"Good night—I'm going home!"

"But, Harry, stop—let's go over to Florence's and have one more drink. What's got into you to-night?"

"The *devil!*" replied Whitmore gruffly, and turning on his heel he walked quickly up into Broadway.

"Well, I believe so!" muttered Livingston, looking in astonishment upon the receding form of his friend, and then slowly taking the same direction.

He had gone but a few steps, when he heard a noise in

the direction taken by Whitmore, which indicated a row. Gus. was not exactly a coward, though not overstocked with bravery, and as he detected the sound of Whitmore's voice in a loud key he hurried on to his assistance.

He found him at the corner just above Florence's, surrounded by a set of fellows who seemed crazy drunk, and who were in fact the same whom we have already seen at the house in Church street.

"So *ho!* try to run over a b'hoy rough-shod would yer!" cried the leader of the gang to Whitmore, who it appeared had offended him in some way.

"Get out of the way, or by Heaven I'll let daylight through you!" said Whitmore, attempting to proceed, and drawing a dirk from his bosom.

"So, you'd stick a feller, would yer!" cried Mose, adding a tremendous oath, "I'll show yer a trick of the Bowery, *I* will!" and in a moment a whizzing sound was heard, as he whirled something in circles around his head.

Whitmore advanced, and crash came the heavy slung-shot down upon his raised arm, and it fell powerless by his side, dropping the knife, for the bone was broken.

"Go it, Mose! Give him hell!" cried the b'hoys, and again the terrible weapon came crashing down upon his head, though with less force, for his hat partly broke the blow. Yet it was very severe, entirely stunning him.

"Hays!" cried the crowd. "Hays, Mose, you've done him!" and the b'hoys made off at full speed.

Livingston arrived in a moment after, and found Whitmore senseless, and bleeding very badly. Summoning the watch, he had him carried to his own rooms, which were near, and called a surgeon.

The latter at once examined his injuries, which were found very severe, and placed his broken arm in splints. The wound on the head, however, had only served to stun him for the time, and within three or four hours he had recovered his senses, enough to know his own situation.

"Curse the luck!" he muttered—"it seems as if the devil was disposed to thwart me in everything just now! How soon can I move, doctor?"

"You ought not to think of it under three weeks, and then with care!" replied the surgeon.

"Three weeks? Damnation!" muttered the libertine fiercely. "If it costs my life, I'll be out in three days!"

"You'll do it at your own risk! Your arm is very badly broken!" said the doctor.

It was now nearly dawn, and Whitmore, calling Gus. Livingston to his side, said in a low whisper,—

"There are four hundred and twenty-five dollars in my pocket, Gus.!"

"Yes," replied that worthy,—"what can I do for you, Harry?"

"Just take two hundred of it around to old Ma'am Swett's, and tell her how I'm fixed. Tell her to keep that bird in the cage safe for me, and I'll be around as soon as I can. The other two hundred and twenty-five you can have!"

"Thank you!" replied Gus., "but what bird do you mean? Not Charley's sister?"

"Yes,—I've got her there, but as you value me and your own life, keep it mum. Don't let it get out, or she may escape me before I am well. Tell old Swett to keep the secret, and she'll be no loser!"

"Certainly I will, but by Jove, Harry, you *are* a genius! Nothing puts you out," said the echo, filled with admiration at the villany of his leader

CHAPTER V.

———

THE appointed evening came for Mrs. Abingdon to again repair to the establishment of Genlis, the Gipsey King. With
woman's tact, she managed to arrange her visit so as to relieve
her husband of any fears which might arise from her absence,
and, moreover, she had, with woman's *unusual* secresy, kept her
husband ignorant of her former visit, and the sight which she
had witnessed.

She hurried to the place where she before had found the
carriage, for her heart yearned to again see her child, even
though it was a shadow or unreal substance. Yet she could not
but think that she had indeed seen her child, and she determined
in this visit to satisfy herself, and to use all means to recover it,
if possible. She had again brought the exorbitant fee demanded
by the gipsey, and was willing to give even much more for the
restoration of her child.

On arriving at the house of the Indian fortune-teller, she
found everything as before, and in the same manner, having paid
her fee, was conducted into the carriage and driven to the house
of Genlis. The same caution was used in introducing her to the
building, and when at last she found herself seated, she heard the
same voice give her the cautions which she had before
received.

"If you would see your child, and know his fate, and where
he now is," said the soft and gentle voice, "be perfectly calm—
watch all the changes on the face of the magic mirror, but utter
not one word or they will vanish for ever. Art thou prepared
for the trial?"

"I am, oh hasten the blessed sight!" murmured the mother,
while her whole frame trembled with agitation.

"You must be more calm—you are too agitated!" said the

voice. "count one thousand calmly, and then remove the bandage from your eyes !"

Nerving herself for the scene, the lady did as she was directed, and when at last she had fulfilled the numbers, she hastily tore the veil from her eyes.

The same scene presented itself to her view, which she had seen before. The pall-like curtain of black velvet which hung at the upper end of the room—the beautiful figure appearing so like an angel, stood in the same place where she had seen it before.

"Oh ! can this be a scene of magic !" she thought, " or am I in a dream ?"

A deep voice by her side caused her to turn quickly, and she trembled, as she again looked upon Genlis, the Gipsey King.

" Thou wouldst again try our skill, lady ?'

" Yes, oh yes, show me my child !"

" Thou shalt see him soon, but I would warn thee not again to dispel the charm, as thou didst before !"

" I will not," murmured the mother, " but, oh ! if it is in your power to show me my child, can you not restore it to me ?"

" Lady, I do not show thee thy child—it is but his magic shadow, yet it will tell thee where he is—and how to regain him !"

" Then he can be found ! Oh ! I would give all I have to press him once more to my breast !"

" Well, lady, I will see where he now is, and I doubt not but magic and gold can recover him for thee !"

Genlis smiled as he said this. Perchance he thought, as we do, that magic and gold are very closely connected in the present day, for gold ever hath a magical effect. Who that owns it, lacketh friends ? What girl, be she ever so ugly, that hath it in abundance, is doomed to linger on husbandless ? Is it not the passport to SOCIETY ? Is it not the mantle of respectability, here in this *republican* land ? In the language of a popular poet, " *it aint nothin' else !*"

After he smiled, Genlis said to the lady :

" The charm is about to commence—be guarded and do not break it !"

She did not respond, but fixed her eyes upon the curtain,

which slowly began to rise, as Genlis waved his wand, and the lovely being that stood near it knelt upon the floor.

First Mrs. A. only looked upon the smooth face of the mirror, then again she saw it overspread with the mist and clouds as before, and suddenly she heard the sound of distant music. It was like that of a military band. She plainly heard the beating drum and clear tones of the bugle, and she remembered then the hour when last she had seen her darling boy.

Suddenly the mist cleared away partially, and through its thin veil she saw a picture which plainly resembled the street where she lived, and she recognised her own house. Then, while the music swelled louder and louder, a company of soldiers appeared marching slowly by, and amid a crowd of children and others who rushed out to see them, she recognised her Willie, his little golden ringlets flowing on the breeze which shook the banners above him. The little fellow followed on, clapping his hands and gazing upon the brilliant display.

The scene was so real, so life-like, that the mother could scarcely believe it was a delusion, but the mist gathered again upon the mirror, and the picture was hidden.

Mrs. Abingdon sighed, and while tears coursed freely down her flushed cheeks, she turned to Genlis. Seeing that she was about to speak, he placed his finger upon his lip as a sign for her to be silent, and then with his wand again pointed to the mirror.

She looked, and another picture was rising in the mist. Her boy was on the upper deck of a steamboat, which was swiftly gliding through bright and placid waters. A tall and beautiful lady was holding him by the hand, and the young child seemed to be gazing out upon the small waves, which danced up and down in the sunlight, making the river look as if it was carpeted with scales of glittering tinsel.

At his feet lay some toys, which he had just dropped, and in his hand he held some candy, which he seemed to have forgotten, as he looked out upon the bright waters.

And the dark-eyed lady who held his other hand, seemed to be gazing tearfully upon the high hills which rose beyond the river side, and scarcely to heed the beautiful child.

The mother felt as if she stood upon the shore all this time ;

she saw the boat pass on. She would have cried out, but her lips seemed glued together; she would have at last beckoned to her child, but her arms seemed as if they were bound, and she was forced, silently, tearfully, to gaze on, until they had passed away from her view, and the boat had vanished up the river, between the lofty Highlands.

Then she raised her hands to her eyes, and an involuntary sob burst from her bosom.

Genlis touched her shoulder, and pointed again to the mirror.

She saw a beautiful country village. There was the neat church, with its tall white spire; the rows of small, neat frame houses, with their white walls and green doors and window blinds; their flower gardens in front, guarded with white picket fences; a scattered store here and there, with specimens of its miscellaneous stock of dry goods and hardware, hung up and stuck around the door. Little children were playing around upon the green in the centre, but Willie was not among them. Grown up girls and ladies were walking to and fro with their simple dresses, and wide-caped sun-bonnets, but Mrs. A. could not recognise the tall, dark-eyed one among them.

She looked around to Genlis to know what was meant by this scene, and he again pointed to the mirror with his wand.

Her glance thus directed to it, found the scene already changed. She saw the interior of a school-house. A large desk stood in the centre of the back part of the room. On either side, along the wall, from this desk to the door, stretched a row of high benches, faced by a row of desks, sloping towards the benches, whereon were seated the largest scholars, the boys on one side, the girls on the other. On the boys' side the desks not only bore many an ink stain, but many a deep cut, evincing the natural disposition which the rising generation of this country have for whittling.

In front of the big scholars' row of benches, was a line of seats adapted to those of a lesser size, and in front of this, one suited for the *abecedarians,* if so we may class the little ones, whose sex could not be distinguished by any difference of dress. But while describing the location of the young folks, we have forgotten to speak of the occupant of the high seat at the large desk, which occupied the central and commanding position at the head of the room. There, in a place where his cold grey eye could at a glance fix itself upon every scholar, sat a man who looked as if the sweat of human kindness had never dampened his dry pale skin. The top of his head was bald, but it was not glossy; the few hairs which were scattered down about his ears and temples, looked like threads of badly rotted and mildewed flax, stuck on for a fringe. His forehead was a concentrated wrinkle, which gathered into a knot just over his nose, making his expression that of a perpetual frown. His features were sharp, and his chin, which appeared to have been shaved very close, to judge from sundry little notches and spots patched by pickings of felt from his hat, was half hidden by the projecting points of his stiff shirt collar, which supported his head on either side, by fitting snugly under his ears. A coat colored butter-nut brown, and patched with black in both the elbows, was buttoned close around his slim form. In one hand he held a long flat ruler of cherry-wood, and near the other lay a large bundle of small tapering hazel switches with the knots cut smoothly off. Behind his ears were sundry quill pens, which doubtless needed mending, and before him lay quite a pile of copy-books, some of them headed with a row of pot-hooks, others yet to suffer with blottings of the beginner.

And this was the schoolmaster upon his throne.

Mrs. A. glanced along the well filled benches, and as her eye ran down the row of little ones, who sat there with their hands crossed in their laps, facing the master, she once more saw her Willie. The poor little fellow did not look as happy as before—his cheeks were pale, and his golden curls had evidently been neglected, he had no mother now to train them into glossy ringlets, and his eye seemed to look upon the pale-faced, cadaverous looking master, with an expression of fear.

The picture was, alas! *very* life-like. Mrs. A. gazed upon it but one moment, not half so long as it has taken us to describe it and then unable to restrain herself longer, cried:

"Oh God! my poor—poor Willie!"

The curtain fell, and she burst into tears.

"Are you satisfied, now, lady?" asked Genlis.

"Oh, tell me what does it mean! Has this been a true picture?" cried Mrs. A. in reply.

"It has," responded Genlis. "The child has evidently been stolen from you!"

"But for what? I never have harmed any one!"

"I cannot say for what reason it was stolen—my art has not revealed that—but it has shown where he is. He is alive and at school in some country village!"

"But can you not find where he is? Oh, if you will but tell me, so that I can recover him, I will bless you all my life!"

"It will cost much money, I fear. My time is precious and my art is a dangerous one here!"

"I do not care. Get my child back, and you shall have money!"

"You will not pay my price!"

"Oh, yes, I will! What is it?"

"Ten thousand dollars!"

The lady looked at the Gipsey with astonishment. "Ten thousand dollars!" she murmured, "will it cost so much?"

"Yes!" replied Genlis, "for I must make a journey!"

"Then I must tell my husband—I cannot get so large a sum except from him!"

"You must get it without his knowledge!" said the cunning Gipsey, who knew that a man's suspicions would be easily aroused, and his credulity be less susceptible than that of a fond and half crazed mother.

"I know not how to do it—yet I will try!" murmured the lady. "Oh, I must rescue my poor boy! How cold and cruel that schoolmaster looked!"

"The time for your interview is over, lady. When you are ready to pursue this search and pay my demand, go to Julia and let her know. One half must be in advance—the other five thousand, when the boy is in your arms!" said Genlis; and without waiting to hear her answer, he proceeded to veil her as before, to prepare her for her return home.

CHAPTER VI.

"Ah, ha! I see you 'ave one ver select companie!" cried our old friend Captain Tobin, as he entered Jack Circle's crib.

The very select company consisted of Black Bill, Jack Murphy, 'Tilda Smith, Harriet Circle, Long Bill, Charley Cooper, and a few more of the "fraternity," who were enjoying a quiet smoke and "summat vet."

"Ah, ha! one ver select companie, Capitan Shack!"

"Ello! Uncle Tommy!" cried old Jack, as he recognised his visitor; "tip us your mauley, my cove! 'ow did you get along with the up-town swells?"

"I 'ave make one ver goot speculacione!" replied the captain. "If zat dam Messieur Matsell 'ave not spot me, I should 'ave make ze forchune of ze whole companie!"

"Wot! Did the old fox smell you out?"

"Yes, by dam, he know ev'ry sing! He see me wiz one of ze up-town ladie in her carriage, and zen he give one such look —by dam, I sink it was time for me to make myself ver scarce, before he find out where I live!"

"Blast his heyes, he's aller's a spyin' round, and a man might as well be in h—l as on the cross in his neighborhood!" growled Black Bill. "Him and old Bowyer and a lot more of the same kidney, spile our trade!"

A general murmur of assent was given by the whole party, which was hushed by Circle, who wanted to know the upshot of the Frenchman's story.

"Did you lift much of a swag?" asked he of Captain Tobin.

"Let me see—I 'ave two brasslet—real glis'n's* in 'em—zat are wors six tousand dollare, ze two; zen I 'ave borrow two

---

* "Pad the hoof,"—to clear out in a hurry, thief's slang. "Thimbles:" watches. "Glistens:" diamonds. "Spot:" to recognise.

ver fine timbles,* one of a ladee—ze ozzare was present me by Messieur Fish-Lawrence; zen I 'ave borrow fifteen hondred dollare in monee!"

"Be jabers, but it's yerself as does the thing up gentale!" cried Mr. Murphy, struck with admiration at the Count's success.

"Ah, if had not been for zat dam Messieur Matsell," said Tobin, with a sigh, "I should 'ave make one ver grand specu lacione, but I knew when he spot* me zat I must pad my hoof!"

"Never mind, Uncle Tommy, you've lifted a fair swagg, arter all!" said Circle.

"Yes, sare; but dam zat Messieur Matsell!" sighed Tobin, "he interrupt me, when I was in one ver interesting *liason*, shust when I was make love to one ladee, who was plentee rish! Ah!—dam zat Messieur Matsell!"

The Frenchman paused and sighed, then bowing very politely to Harriet Circle, he said :

"If you please, Mademoiselle—will you make for me one of your shin cock-tail superbe?"

"I won't do nothin' else, Uncle Tommy!" replied the girl, and hurried away to prepare his gin cock-tail, while old Circle and the rest of the company crowded around to see the plunder which the Frenchman had brought.

The latter was now the hero of the evening—his praise was in every one's mouth, and old Circle was so delighted, that he shouted to "Arriet," to bring up "summat vet" for the entire party, at his expense.

She came up in a few moments, accompanied by Frank Hennock, who had just arrived.

Frank had now gained a position, which made him "some-body" in the crowd, and his arrival was noticed by all of the rest. The party was at the same time augmented by the arrival of another of the gang, Big Lize.

Her face was flushed, as if she had been drinking,—and her eyes were flashing with anger or excitement.

"Ello, Lize! What's up now?" cried old Circle, as he noticed her excited looks upon entering.

* See Note on preceding page

"Give me some gin!" she muttered almost fiercely,—"give me some gin, I'm in trouble!"

"What, 'aven't you 'eard nuthin' 'o the gal yet?" asked Cooper, who had evidently seen her since the loss of Angelina.

"No,—I've been back to that crib in Greenwich street, and it wasn't her as was there arter all!" cried the woman, emptying a glass of gin at a single draught.

"What're ye patterin' habout?" asked old Circle.

"Nuthin' as concerns the bizness!" replied Cooper; "it's honly some private trouble of Lize's!"

"Vel, vot is it? Can't we 'elp her?"

"Not's I see! She's lost the run o' a cousin o' hers, a poor young gal, as she'd taken a likin' to!"

"Oh's that all? I didn't know but she'd been up afore his 'onor!" said Jack Circle.

"D'ye think I'd care for that, you noddy?" said Lize, spitefully. "I don't care no more for his 'onor than I do for you, and that aint much; but if I don't find that 'ere poor gal afore I'm much older, I'll burn half o' this town up!"

"An' be jabers but a *summery* way that 'ud be to find her!" cried Jack Murphy, "there 'ud be warm weather if ye wor to do it!"

"I don't want none o' your jokes, but I've a favor to ask of you all!" cried Lize.

"Then spake out, as the young 'un said to the cat, when he pinched her tail!" cried Mr. Murphy.

"I want you all when you're on the tramp, to keep a look-out for this girl, my cousin. She's about sixteen year old, and very 'an'some!"

"Then there's no family resemblance!" said Mr. Murphy, rather ungallantly.

Lize, however, did not heed his remark, but continued:

"She's got bright brown hair all in curls—blue eyes, that look as if they were made for an angel, and is pale and thin a little now, cause she's seen trouble!"

Frank Hennock stepped up to Lize, and was about to speak, when she added:

"I'll give a hundred dollars to any one of ye that'll find her for me!"

Frank paused when he heard this, and repressed the remark he was about to make. He thought that he recognised in the description, the young girl who was at his master's, but he determined to see Lize alone, ask her some questions, and then, if his supposition was correct, he could quietly pocket the reward which Lize offered.

At that moment the usual signal was given, and another person entered from outside. It was Carlton, and he was alone.

He smiled as he saw Tobin, and said:

"You did very well up town, eh, captain?"

"Yes, Sare, but dam zat Messieur Matsell. He spot me, and stop my speculacione—an' it is not ze first time he 'ave done so!"

"Yes, I heard of it, I just saw young Fitz-Lawrence, who was in a devil of a stew, blowing up Sam Selden for introducing you!"

"Ah, ha! What did Messieur Selden say for one excuse!"

"He told the young fellow that you had excellent letters, that you had imposed on him too, and all that; smoothed it over as well as he could!"

"But 'ow did zis young Fish-Lawrence find out so soon zat I was not a Count, eh?"

"Why the officers have been at Fitz-Lawrence's, and at your boarding-house, and have found out the whole affair, except *who* the Count was, and what has become of the plunder!"

"Ah ha! Zat dam Messieur Matsell, he work ver sharp! I was right no to go back to my room after I 'ave see him, for I sink he know de ladee zat I was ride wiz?"

"To be sure, and he went to Mrs. Klawke to get on your track!"

"Zen I was right again! I get her to set me down, before I got to her house! Eh bien, Messieur Matsell, I 'ave been too mooch for you zis time!" and the Frenchman rubbed his hands with glee, as he thought of his escape.

"Well, Mr. Carlton, wot habout that 'ere lay. Isn't it time we was a doin suthin? If the boys don't 'ave some work afore long they'll forget 'ow! There's nuthin like keepin' their 'ands in!"

"That's true, Jack," replied Carlton, "you may look out for the first rainy night. But have you picked out a place to stow the goods away in?"

"Yes, 'Til Smith's dad—the old city Bank covey, has a snuggery up town, as 'll do."

"Well, that's settled now; what about old Precise?"

"You may crack his crib as soon as you like!" said Frank, stepping forward, "I'm tired of stoppin' there, and I'm afraid there'll be apparent reasons for my leaving before long at any rate!"

"Why, what's up?" asked old Circle.

"Don't be afther axin the young gintleman questions as makes 'im blush!" cried Jack Murphy, "didn't he say the reasons would soon be *apparent*, when only his modesty kept him from saying out bouldly, that it 'ud be 'imself that 'ud be a-*parent!*"

"He's hit it!" said Frank, "and the sooner I get out of the house, the better I'll be pleased!"

"Ow much of a swag can we lift?" asked Black Bill.

"Why some ready tin—a set of silver—gold watch and chain, a little jewelry, and some duds, that's all!"

"Arn't the young 'oman saved up suthin?" asked Long Bill.

"Yes—but I'm principled against taking her earnings! It's all she's got, and she'll need it before long!"

"The young 'un's right!" said old Circle, then turning to Carlton, he asked:

"'Ave you tried the check?"

Carlton replied, by throwing down a roll of bank notes upon the table.

"Them's the tickets!" said Circle, as he gathered up the lot. "Don't you think we can try it on agin?"

"We might for a small figure!" replied the gambler.

"Then, young 'un, spose you do us another check!" said Circle, addressing himself to Frank.

"For how much?" asked the young villain.

"It won't do to risk over five hundred!" said Carlton.

"I'll give it to you to-morrow!" said Frank; "but when are we to divide and share off?"

"Next Sunday!" replied Circle, "that is, if all 'ands are hagreed!"

A general assent was given, and Frank Hennock then asked, when he might expect a visit from the gang at his master's.

"I've left that 'ere lay to Black Bill and Jack Murphy!" said Circle.

"When will you be up ?" asked Frank of these *gentlemen.*

" At our airliest convayniance, my honey !" said Jack, "and we hope the ould gintilman wont throuble himself to sit up for us !"

" But *when* will you come ?" asked Frank impatiently, addressing himself to Black Bill.

"The first nasty night, when we can wear mufflers and get along without running over the coppers. I reckon it 'll be habout the change of the moon—it's sure to rain then !"

" Well, I'll be on the look-out !—shall I leave the lower door unbolted ?"

"No—there's so many bloody hout-siders cruisin' habout, they might get ahead ov hus—besides, I'd rayther go in at the winder. It's more legitimate !"

" Well, have it your own way—but I'd like to make a scene after you're all through," said Frank, "just to keep up appearances on my side. After you've lifted all you can, and got clear, I'd like to make a fuss, and shoot at some imaginary thief !"

"Oh, yes, so's to gammon the gov'nor ! That's all right, and it 'ud make it safer for the young 'un !" said Circle, approvingly.

The plans for robbing the Broadway store and the house of Mr. Precise were now duly canvassed and discussed by the whole party, and the men picked out who were to attend to the business. Several other lays were also mentioned, but these were to be deferred until the two first had been attended to.

" I wonder 'ow Genlis is adoin' with his lay ?" asked Circle of Carlton.

" First rate—let him have his own way in that !" said the latter, "he's keen !"

" Aye, you're more than 'alf right there !" said Circle, "and now let's all take summat vet !"

Finding that the business was over, Frank now thought of his promise to be home early, and taking advantage of a moment when the rest were clustering around the table where the liquor was, he asked Big Lize to go out with him. She at first refused, but he hinted at his knowledge of the girl, and she immediately hurried out with him.

CHAPTER VII.

In a room of that same mysterious house, which we have already described—the one where Albert Shirley met poor Mary Sheffield, and where we have before seen Mrs. Carlton—sat the last named lady.

Her beautiful face was flushed with excitement. Her eyes were red—she had evidently been weeping—and her form seemed to quiver with agitation. She started at every sound which she heard, and seemed to be anxiously awaiting the appearance of some one.

Suddenly a step was heard ascending the stairs—the door flew open, and Cooly entered.

"Charles, dear Charles!" she cried, as she sprang into his arms—"I'm so glad to see you—I've had a terrible scene with my husband!"

"Yes, so your note told me—but does he know of our intimacy?"

"Yes, he told me all, and named you,—I denied it, but I know he has found it out!"

"The devil he has! what is to be done?" cried Cooly, turning pale.

"We must fly, dear Charles!" said the lady, not noticing his pallor.

"Fly! where to, or how? I have no means of leaving!"

"I am prepared for that. Here are two thousand dollars, which I took from a drawer in my bureau, where he left it!" replied the ready-witted and fond woman. "We can leave the country with that, or go out west!"

Cooly did not reply. Things had evidently taken a turn which he did not like.

"Don't you think it'll all blow over, if we separate for a while, Hannah?" asked he.

"Blow over!" exclaimed she, in surprise—"you know little of Henry Carlton if you dream of such a thing! He never will forgive you or me—and your *life* alone will satisfy him!"

"But, Hannah, you know I go prepared; besides this, he would not dare to try to attack me here, in the crowded city, where policemen are so thick!"

"*Dare*—Charles? He dare do anything! You don't know him as I do! Will you go with me or not?"

"Why, Hannah, really —— I ——"

"Answer me, sir, at once! Let it be yes or no!" cried Mrs. C. sternly.

"Why, Hannah, my business ——!"

"Charles Cooly, don't try to form an excuse. Your business is worth nothing, and you're in debt now. I offer you two thousand dollars, to leave all and go with me to some place where we are not known. Here, take the money!" and she handed him a pocket-book.

"But, Hannah, what is the use? I should be called a coward by all my friends—I should have to leave ——!"

"*Leave?* Do you talk of *leaving* anything?" cried the lady in a bitter tone. "Do you leave two children whom you love as you do your own soul—do you leave every luxury which heart can desire, as I do? Stop, Charles Cooly, don't speak! I've something to say, now, and I *will not* be interrupted till I have said it!

"You met me, and won me away from a fond and trusting husband—you made me love you, as *I*, only I can love! You have brought me into that fearful shadow from which I can never escape, for when a woman's fair fame is once lost, it can never be regained. Our intimacy is known, my reputation is blasted for ever, by and for you. I have given up honor, wealth, children—all—all for you, and now *dare* you stand there and say you will not fly with me, at least beyond the persecutions of my husband?"

Cooly turned pale as death while he listened to her eloquent and bitter gush of language, and yet he thought that he never before had seen her look so beautiful as she did then, with her eyes flashing, her face flushed, and her form swelling in **every** muscle.

"Why do you not answer—will you go with me?" she continued.

"Give me a little time to think of it, Hannah!" said he.

"I would not thus have answered you!" she said, scornfully. "No, Charles, had I been in your place, and were you in mine, we would, even now, be speeding to some distant spot, where we could be happy!"

"But, Hannah, this has come upon me unexpectedly, and I was unprepared for it!"

"Unprepared? Why, Charles, how often I have warned you that I had a watchful and dangerous husband! You ought to have been ready for this, as I was—but when will you give me your answer?"

"In a day or two!" replied Cooly.

"In a day or two! Why, Charles—a day or two hence ought to find us hundreds of miles from here. No,—you must answer within two hours—and mark me, if you desert me now, I will *hate* you with all the fervor with which I have loved you. *Beware!*"

The warm-blooded and impetuous woman turned and left the room.

"Well, this is a devil of a scrape!" muttered Cooly, as he turned towards the door.

"Yes!" said a deep voice close by his side, and he turned red and white alternately, and trembled in every joint as he felt a hand laid heavily upon his shoulder.

The speaker was Sam Selden, who, hidden by the curtains of the heavy mahogany bedstead, had been a witness to this interview, unknown to both parties.

Cooly quickly put his hand inside of his vest, as if to grasp a concealed weapon.

"Pshaw! keep cool! Don't go to drawing anything on me!" said the gambler, fixing his dark eyes upon the pallid face of Cooly, "be sensible, and let us arrange this little matter!"

"What have you got to do with it?" asked Cooly, a little more assured, when he saw no sign of attack made by Selden.

"A good deal!" replied the gambler. "I'm Harry Carlton's bosom friend—he loves his wife yet, unworthy as she is. I have heard her proposal—saw her give you the two thousand dollars.

Now all I have to say is this,—quit her, and leave the city without her, and you may keep the money !"

" I will quit her, but not the city,—and as to the money, you may take it back to Carlton !" replied Cooly.

" You're a fool !" said Selden impatiently—" if you stay here, Harry Carlton 'll kill you !"

" No, he wont—and all I'll do is to give up the woman !" said Cooly.

" Then you will *not* leave the place ?"

" No,—there is the money—take it to Carlton, and tell him his wife is as much to blame as I am !"

" Will you write to her, and let me take the note, and say in it that you are done with her for ever ?"

" Yes, and glad to get rid of her so easy.   She has a devil of a temper, and begins to be troublesome !" replied Cooly.

The gambler rang the bell.   In a moment the lady of the house came to the door.

" Wine, gentlemen ?" she asked, in a tone and with a manner that did not evince any surprise at the appearance of Selden, who she knew was in the house, but had supposed to be in another room.

" No," replied Selden, with his usual politeness, " but writing materials, if you please, Madame !"

In a few moments they were brought, and Cooly wrote a note, which was dictated by Selden.

" Now, all I have to say is, that you'd better keep clear of Carlton, and let *her* alone for the future !" said Selden, as he pocketed the note, and also the money which Cooly had returned.

Cooly left the room without a reply.   Selden smiled when he was gone.

" So far, so well !" he muttered.   " I wonder how she'll like this note," and he read over the letter of Cooly.   " I reckon she'll wish she hadn't crossed Sam Selden's wishes !"

Then wrapping his handsome Spanish cloak around him, the gambler left the room.

CHAPTER VIII.

———

ONE hour after the last scene, Mr. and Mrs. Carlton were alone in that neat little parlor, above the gambling hell, which overlooked the graveyard.

He was paler than usual, and much agitated, while she was as calm and composed as if her bosom never had harbored a thought other than a pure and faithful wife should think.

"I am sorry you are so jealous, Henry!" said she, in her usual sweet and musical tone. "Some one has been telling tales of me—to set you against me!"

The husband did not reply, but paced up and down the room angrily. A moment after a knock was heard at the door.

"Who's there?" asked Carlton, sternly.

"Selden!"

"Ah! come in, Sam!" cried Carlton, recognising his friend's voice.

The handsome gambler entered, and as he did so, Mrs. C. started to retire into the bed-room beyond.

"Stay a moment, if you please, madam!" cried Selden. "I have a note here, which I was requested to deliver to you!"

The lady returned, and taking the note from his hand glanced at the superscription. She trembled as she did so, and while the blood rushed into her face, she cried:

"Where did you get this, sir?"

"The writer gave it to me a short time since!" he replied. "I met him at a house in ——— street, where he told me he had just parted with a lady!"

"Oh God! can he be such a villain!" she gasped, as she sank back into a seat.

"Read the note, madam, it may require an answer!" said Carlton, who, from a single look given by Selden, seemed to comprehend the case.

"Thank you, sir, for reminding me of it—it may!" said she, in a sarcastic tone, recovering her calmness by a strong effort, and rising from her seat.

There was not a tremor in her hand as she unfolded the note, not a quiver of her lip, as she read every word of its contents. Yet while she read it, the blood forsook her face, her lips became pale and bloodless.

Twice did she read each word in that note. Then slowly she tore it up, and when it was in scraps she threw them on the floor, and placed her small foot upon them.

"Have you seen the contents of that note?" she asked of Selden.

"He wrote it in my presence, and bade me bring to your husband these two thousand dollars!" replied the gambler, handing Carlton the money.

"Where did this money come from, Sam?" asked Carlton.

"He need not tell you—I will!" cried the pale wife; "I took it from the bureau, and gave it to a false coward, to pay his expenses and mine to some distant land!"

"You gave it to Charles Cooly?"

"I did; and the wretch has now spurned it and me from him! may God Almighty *curse him!*"

"Stop, Hannah, stop!" said Carlton, with mock gentleness; "you forget that he is your *lover!*"

"*Lover?* oh God! if the burning hate that I feel for him could rest one moment on his heart, it would shrivel it like fire! Henry Carlton, if you are a man, if you ever loved me, go and *kill* him!"

"And get myself hung, Hannah? no, no, I can't oblige you in that; and, besides, what harm has he done me?"

"*Only* seduced your wife, sir! *only* made a vile adultress of the mother of your children—that is *all!*" cried the maddened woman.

"Why, Hannah, you surprise me! did you not, a short time since, vow by all that was good on earth and holy in heaven, that you were pure, and true to me?"

"Yes, and I perjured myself for him—for the coward, who has so basely deserted her whom he has ruined!"

" And so you think he deserves punishment?" continued the husband.

" Yes, *death !*" hoarsely cried the wife.

" Would *you* kill him ?"

" I—I ? oh God ! I could not !" murmured she.

" And yet he would do more than kill you !"

" Yes, yes ! Henry Carlton, I have done wrong, but hear me; you have been at fault. I loved you devotedly once, but you neglected me. Night after night you stood before your gaming table ; day after day you spent with the companions whom you have gathered around you. This *thing*, I will not call him man, met me in a sad and unguarded moment, when you were away. He saw that I was sad and lonely, and he *pitied* me. That *pity* has been my ruin. Had not your neglect made me an object of pity, I would have still been as true to you as the sun is to its course !"

The gambler listened to her words, and his voice trembled as he turned to Selden and said :

" Sam, leave us alone a little while !"

After the door was closed, Carlton turned to his wife, and she noticed that his eyes were moist.

" Hannah," said he, " you have spoken truly. Much of this has been my fault. I love you yet, and I will forgive you when—when that wretch is dead !"

" I do not ask forgiveness," she replied. " I have wronged myself and my children as much as I have injured you. But as for *him*—he must not live to glory in my shame !"

" He shall not," replied the gambler slowly, but firmly. Then he added :

" Hannah, I have a favor to ask of you !"

" Speak on—I am your slave henceforth, Henry !"

" No, Hannah, do not speak so !" replied he kindly. " I will bury the past. We will both do better in future !"

Tears came from his eyes as he spoke. How strange it was that one so hardened in deep and calculating villany as he, could weep : could be possessed of some of those softer and more tender feelings of human nature, placed in his bosom perchance to contrast with his other attributes, as we sometimes see the violet and rose peep out on a barren mountain side, in the **very** shadow of the grim black rocks.

But he brushed these away and said :

" I want you to write a note, or send a message to Cooly, Hannah !"

" What, Henry ?"

" It will be the last you need ever send, Hannah ; he *dies* to-morrow night !"

The woman looked up in her husband's eyes, and she knew he meant what he said.

" What message shall I send ?" she asked.

" Tell him that you must have a few minutes conversation to-morrow evening. Ask him to meet you and walk with you a little way !"

" I will send the word," she replied. "Retire into the bed-room, and I will ring the bell for Eliza !"

Carlton obeyed, and Mrs. C. rang a little bell which lay upon her table. In a moment the mulatto girl came in.

" Eliza," said the lady, "I want you to go and see Mr. Cooly for me !"

" Yes, Mistress !"

" I want you to tell him I have received his note, and that it is all right, but I *must* see him once more. Tell him I ask it for the *last* time, and that he must take a short walk with me to-morrow night !"

" Yes, Mistress !"

" And be careful—let no one hear you deliver the message !"

The servant disappeared on her errand, and Carlton again came forward.

" You have done right, Hannah. I will now make my ar-rangements !"

" To punish him ?" she asked with a shudder.

" Yes," he replied, "I shall not rest till it is done. Remem-ber, Hannah, no feeling for him ! He has deserted and spurned you away from him !"

" It is true !" she murmured bitterly—"I will not pity him—but must I aid in his death ?"

" Yes, you must get him into a good place. You must get

him off alone, for the coward keeps a crowd around him all the time, and there is no other way of getting him alone !"

"Do as you will—I am your slave now !" said she sadly.   "He *deserves* death !"

"He shall have it, Hannah—yet we must act very cautiously to avoid the law !"

"Will you kill him ?" she asked.

"No."

"Then it is Sam Selden !" she said.

"No, both of us might be suspected.   I have chosen one on whom suspicion cannot rest.   Even you will not know by whom the deed is done.   I have all my plan laid, and it cannot fail !"

"It ought not—yet—"

"Yet, what ?   Why this trembling and agitation, Hannah ? Look at the paper which lies at your feet—did his hand tremble when he wrote that ?"

"No, nor shall mine again !" replied Mrs. C.   "But leave me for a while, Henry ; I will grow calm—desperately calm !"

"I will, but first, Hannah, take this as a token of reconciliation !"

Mrs. C. shuddered as she felt the pressure of his lips.   He had evidently ceased to be an object of either love or respect with her—for when a woman's heart is once alienated, it can never return to its allegiance and former fondness.   Like a flower with its stem half-broken off, it may linger on a little while with the appearance of freshness, but it never can regain its original strength and beauty.

CHAPTER IX.

Mr. Shirley, the seducer of the unhappy Mary Sheffield, was seated in his elegantly furnished sitting-room, listening to music from the lips of his daughter, a beautiful young girl, who accompanied herself with rare taste on a piano.

Mr. Shirley had finished his day's business, dined comfortably, and now sat there in his dressing-gown and slippers, as carelessly as if his miserable victim, poor Mary, had never existed. Had he forgotten her? It would appear so, if one might judge from his smiling face and self-satisfied look.

"That last song was very well sung, child!" he said, as his daughter arose from her piano, and coming to his side, pressed her fair pure lips to his high brow.

"I think our Constance is improving in her music!" said Mrs. Shirley, a pale care-worn looking lady, who seemed to be older than he.

"Yes, and in beauty too!" said the proud father.

"Beauty is a dangerous possession!" said the mother sadly. "It has been the ruin of many a poor girl!"

A sudden cloud seemed to cross the brow of Mr. Shirley, but he shook it off, and said, gently:

"You're always moralizing, my dear. If our daughter does not benefit by your teachings, it will be her own fault!"

The reply of Mrs. Shirley was cut short by the entrance of a servant, who brought in a note.

"This was just left, Sir," said the servant, "by a man who said it must be delivered in haste!"

Mr. Shirley opened it, and turned as pale as death when he read it.

"What is the matter, dear father?" cried his daughter, noticing his agitation.

"Albert, you have bad news there!" cried his wife.

" No, no, only some perplexing business," he replied.

" Can you not tell me what it is ?" asked the lady, sadly ; "if you have any trouble or perplexity, who should share it but your wife ?"

" It is nothing, Cordelia," he replied—" only a friend of mine is in some trouble—I must go down town and see him !"

" You will not be gone long, dear Father !" said the daughter, "we shall be very lonesome till you return !"

" I'll soon be home, my pet !" said Mr. Shirley, kissing her, and then he hurried to change his dress, preparatory to going out.   In a few moments he had gone forth, and he was hurrying as fast as he could to obey a summons which was contained in the note which he had just received—a summons which he *dared* not disobey.

And what was that summons? Let the note itself say. Mr. Shirley, in his haste and agitation, had dropped it upon the floor when he went out, instead of thrusting it in a side pocket as he thought he had.

Constance picked it up a moment after he had left, and as it was open, noticed the writing.

" In what a beautiful hand it is written, mother !" she said, " it must be from a lady !"

The mother glanced at the note carelessly, but the first four or five words attracted her attention, and she could not take her eyes from it.   She turned pale, but she read on.

The note was as follows :

" My dear Mr. Shirley,
    " Mary Sheffield is very low, and I am afraid she will not live the night through.   The *operation* is over, but it has been a fearful time. She is perfectly sensible, and insists upon see-ing you immediately. She bids me say to you, that she will not live to see the sun rise, and I fear that she speaks but too truly. You had better come, for if she dies, I wish to consult you upon the disposition of the body. It is a bad case, and if the police were to get hold of it, both you and I would be in a bad scrape. We cannot get over this as easy as we did with Jane, the bindery girl. Bring some money with you.
                " In haste, truly yours,
                        " Caroline L. Sitstill,
                            " No. —— Greenwich St."

Mrs. Shirley read every word, and then gazed upon that note for a long, long minute, ere she spoke.

Then she fell upon her knees, and with her clasped hands pressed to her brow, murmured:

"Oh God! is it so! was it for this I have been so neglected! and must my poor daughter suffer for his wickedness!"

She dropped the note to the floor, and her daughter, who was terror-stricken by her mother's strange conduct, snatched it up, and cried:

"What is the matter, dear mother? What is there so terrible in this note? It frightened father, and now you are in tears and agony! Tell me, mother, tell me!"

"Nothing, dear Constance, nothing!" replied her mother, trying to calm herself. "Go and tell the coachman to put the horses to the carriage. I am going out!"

"You'll let me go with you, mother?"

"No, child, I cannot. I must go alone!"

"Mother, there is something very strange in all this! Please let me read that note!"

"No, Constance, you must not. I will take care of it!" replied the mother, taking it, and putting it in her bosom. "Now do go and call the carriage!"

The young girl obeyed, but tears were glistening in her eyes as she went. There was a mystery in all this which she could not understand.

The carriage was called, and in a very short time Mrs. Shirley was driving to the same place where her husband had gone. He, having stepped into the first hack he met, had already reached the house where his suffering victim was dying.

He was met by Mrs. Sitstill at the door.

"Is she alive?" he asked, as he entered.

"Yes, but very low. Walk up!" replied the woman, leading the way into a second story back room, where, upon a splendid couch lay a pale, ghastly looking creature, whom Shirley recognised as her who had been so beautiful, poor Mary Sheffield. Her features were now distorted with pain, her eyes were sunken, and the color had fled from her lips and cheeks.

"So, you have come, Albert!" she whispered huskily; "I wanted to see you before I died!"

"You will not die, Mary," he replied, in a choked tone; "the worst is over now!"

"No, Albert—the worst is *not* over! For me and for you the worst is yet to come! I shall die in a few hours, but even then the worst is not over. Albert Shirley,—there is a *hell* for both of us! For you, there may yet be joy on earth—you may have time given you for repentance—but you will *never* forget me!"

Shirley trembled and quivered as if his heart already felt the torments of hell.

"Come close to me, Albert!" said the dying girl,—"come close to me, and take my hand. I want to talk to you. I have *loved* you, Albert, and I love you yet, though you have deceived, ruined, *murdered* me, soul and body!"

The man groaned, but did not speak—he felt even then a deeper agony than she.

"I have yet one favor to ask, before I die," she continued, "it is, that you'll take care of my poor mother, and aid her. Do not leave her to the cold charity of the alms-house, or in her helpless old age permit her to be a wandering beggar in the streets. If it had not been for you, Albert, I should yet be the happy girl I was, and be living to support and take care of her!"

Her words cut him to the very soul—for they were true. He could not gainsay a single one of them.

"I will take care of her!" he replied.

"Then, Albert, I will forgive you all the wrong you have done me. But do not let her or the world know the cause of my death—bury me secretly, and do not let my name be blasted with the shadow of this shame!"

"You will not die, Mary,—do cheer up,—the worst is over!" said he, trying to cheer her up even against his own fears, for he felt that she was indeed dying.

"No,—I feel that death is laying his cold hand upon me!" she murmured, "but I do not wish to live—yet I am not fit to die!"

Suddenly a noise was heard at the door, the sound of footsteps on the staircase was heard, and Shirley shook in every limb, for he recognised the voice of his wife. The servant who had admitted her, supposing her to be a patient who needed the services of Madame S., now found out the error too late, and was trying to persuade her that Mr. Shirley was not there. Madame S. hurried to the door, but as she opened it, the wife saw her husband, and calling his name, rushed up the stairs.

"Let her come!" said Mr. Shirley, mournfully,—"I deserve it all!"

"Where is this Mary Sheffield—where is the wanton who has seduced a husband from his home?" she shrieked, as she rushed into the room.

But she hushed and stood aghast, as she looked upon the pallid face of the dying girl.

"Is that your wife, Albert?" murmured Mary, looking at Mrs. S.

The unhappy man groaned his brief reply.

"Come near to me, lady—I can do you no harm—I am dying!" she murmured.

Mrs. Shirley shuddered, but advanced and took the hand of the dying girl.

"I little thought, lady, that *he* was married, when I gave *him* my love!" she said faintly. "You will forgive me—he told me that he was alone, that no one had a right to his love."

The wife looked at her guilty husband.

"It is true—too true!" he murmured—"Oh, may God forgive me!"

"Amen, even as I do!" feebly added Mary; and then she turned her eyes upon the already tearful face of Mrs. Shirley, and said:

"Forgive me, lady! I wronged you without knowing it!"

"I do! I do!" cried the lady, bursting into tears. "Oh, Albert, what have you done!"

"Damned myself eternally!" groaned the unhappy man.

"Oh, do not say so! Live to do her justice, and to repent!" moaned Mary, and then gasping for breath, she added:

"Albert, take care of——my mother!"

One more gasp, and one attempt to speak—and her breath passed away, while yet the hand of her seducer's wife was clasped in her own. Her last look was upon him, her last word was the name of her poor mother.

28

And this was the last of poor Mary Sheffield—she who was known as the "Pretty Cigar Girl!"

She had been dead scarcely a moment, when Madame Sitstill, in a business-like way, as if she was used to such work, proceeded to close her eyes. Then obeying a sign from Shirley, she left him and his wife alone in the room.

"Oh, Albert, this is dreadful!" murmured the wife. "She's dead!"

"Yes, and I have murdered her!" groaned the conscience-stricken husband. "Cordelia, I have sinned deeply—I have wronged you—but for our daughter's sake, forgive me!"

"For her sake, I will, Albert, if you can forgive yourself—but I can never banish the memory of this night! Yet we will never speak of it again. Arrange for this poor girl's burial, and let us go home, our carriage is at the door!"

The merchant called Madame Sitstill in, and told her that whatever draft she made for burial expenses, should be paid on presentation to him.

"We cannot manage this affair in the usual way!" said Madame S. "The girl is so well known, that her death will be inquired into—but I have a plan that I think will do. Do you keep quiet whatever you may hear. I will attend to all, and on to-morrow I shall expect to have my draft for one thousand dollars cashed!"

"It shall be done!" said Mr. Shirley; then turning to his wife, he asked:

"How came you to know of this, and how did you trace me here?"

She took the letter which he had dropped, from her bosom, and handed it to him.

"I was careless, but, Cordelia, it is for the best. I could not have borne this terrible secret alone—it would have killed me!"

They turned and took a last look at poor Mary as she lay there so white and cold. Her face was calm when she died.

The distortion had passed away, and a smile seemed to have frozen there. Her hands were crossed upon her breast, and much of her remarkable beauty seemed left to her.

They took one last look, then turned away, and soon their carriage rattled from before the door of that terrible house.

Albert Shirley, or the *reality* of our shadow, is yet living; but the memory of that fearful night never will leave him. It haunts his dreams at night; it burdens his soul by day. Poor Mary! She is indeed avenged.

CHAPTER X.

———

It was the morning after Mrs. Abingdon's visit to Genlis. Mrs. A. and her husband were seated at their breakfast table. Both of them looked pale and care-worn.

"Annie," said Mr. A., "you have some secret in your bosom, which you will not confide to me !"

"A secret, Edward !" she replied, in a tone of surprise.

"Yes, dear Annie, one that disturbs you even in your dreams ! It is wronging me not to confide in me !"

"I *do* confide in you, Edward !"

"In *all* things, Annie ? Is there *nothing* that you hide from me ?"

The young wife colored up. She could not tell a lie, and yet she had sworn to Genlis not to reveal her visits.

"Speak, Annie !" said her husband, impatiently. "There is something strange in this conduct !"

"What ! you are not jealous of me, Edward ?"

"No, Annie, God forbid that I should be ; I would not be thus calm if I were, but I know that you have something that troubles you, which you are studiously concealing from me !"

"How do you know it, Edward ?"

"You have unconsciously informed me of it ; I passed a sleepless night, and all the night you were murmuring about some one whom you called *Genlis !*"

The young wife started at this name.

"Who is he ?" asked the husband.

"Edward, I cannot tell you !" she replied.

"Cannot tell me, Annie ? you certainly wish to quarrel with me. Your conduct is unaccountable !"

"I acknowledge it, Edward ; yet if you *will* be angry with me, I cannot help it !"

"You acknowledge that you have a secret which you are keeping from me !"

MYSTERIES AND MISERIES OF NEW YORK.

"Yes, one which I dare not reveal; but it does not concern your honor as a husband, or my duty as a wife!"

"Annie, this must be explained!" said Mr. A., sternly. "Who is this Genlis—what is he?"

"I cannot tell you, Edward!"

"Annie, you *must!* I have never before assumed this tone, but now you force me to do so. I demand this secret!"

"Edward, I have *sworn* not to reveal it!"

"To whom, and for what?"

"To Genlis, and to recover our poor lost boy!"

"Yes, you murmured of him in your sleep, and spoke of a steamboat and a schoolmaster!"

"I was dreaming of the pictures!"

"What pictures, Annie? You will drive me mad with anxiety. Once more, I *demand* this secret of you!"

"Edward, I cannot reveal it!" said the wife, in a firm, sad tone.

"Very well, *Mrs.* Abingdon! I'll see if I cannot find it out in some way. I'll find out this Genlis, if he be in this city, and I'll force the secret from him, even if I have to cut it out of his heart!" cried the husband, angrily.

Mrs. A. burst into tears, but did not answer, while her husband arose from the table, and paced up and down the floor with a heavy, irregular step.

"Fine times!" he continued; "very fine times, when my wife can have *secrets* involving the names of other men, and keep them from me!"

"Edward," said his wife, as she heard this remark, "you will be sorry for this base and unfounded insinuation!"

"And you, madam, ought already to be sorry for having sworn to another man to keep a secret from your husband!"

"Oh, Edward, you wrong me! God in heaven knows that you do!"

"*Perhaps* so, madam. But I've a few questions to ask you. Have I not always been a fond and faithful husband to you?"

"You have, Edward!"

"Has there been a desire of your's ever mentioned which I have not complied with?"

"No, Edward, no! I have no complaint to make!"

"Have you ever known me to withhold from you a single secret, even to the minutest item of my daily business?"

"No!" sobbed the wife.

"That is all; I wished to know if I had fulfilled my duty to you as a fond and true husband!"

"You have, Edward; but do not ask of me this secret!"

"I shall not, madam!" replied the husband, in a slow, calm tone, which betokened his mind to be verging on desperation. "I am about to leave you—I will trouble you no more. You may send for Mr. Genlis to help you keep your secret!"

As he said this, he took his hat from the stand, and turned towards the door.

In a moment, his sobbing wife was on her knees before him, clinging to his form.

"Oh! Edward, for the love of heaven do not treat me so! I do not deserve this—indeed I do not!" she sobbed in broken accents, while she clasped his hands and deluged them with tears.

The husband tried to be sternly calm. He turned away his head, but his lips quivered, and moisture gathered in his eyes.

"Oh! Edward, for the love you bear our poor lost boy, do not leave me in anger! Oh! have mercy upon me! I have *not* wronged you!" cried the unhappy wife.

"The secret!" said he in a low, husky tone, for he was almost choked with emotion.

"Oh! do not go from me—I will tell you all!" she sobbed.

"Rise—do not kneel!" said he, and as he bent down to raise her up, she felt hot tears gush from his eyes upon her face.

"Oh! God, Edward, would you have left me?"

"Annie, I was crazed with suspicion. What is this secret?"

"Sit down, and be calm—I will tell you all. God forgive me for breaking my oath!"

The young wife now revealed to her husband all that had happened, from her first visit to the Indian woman, to the last night's scene.

"Oh! forgive me, Annie, how much I wronged you! You are an angel!" cried the husband, when he had heard all, and with passionate fondness he kissed her pouting lips.

"I thought you would be sorry, for having been so foolish as to be jealous of me !" she replied, with a smile ; "but now that I have told you all, Edward, what is to be done ? Shall we give this man ten thousand dollars ?"

"It is a very large sum, Annie, and he has evidently stolen the child. I do not believe in his magic. That is all humbug !"

"Oh ! Edward, you would not say so, if you had seen all that I have seen !"

"I mean to see it, and him too, Annie. I'll *force* him to restore the child ! He has misled you by his ideas of magic, and you have already given him a thousand dollars !"

"Yes, Edward ! but I thought I could regain our poor Willie by it !"

"True, Annie, and I do not blame you. You were deluded —but you did one sensible thing !"

"What was that, Edward ?"

"Cutting off the cord from the tassel in the hackney-coach. It may lead to the detection of the whole villany. Why did you do it ?"

"I hardly remember. I believe a thought came into my head, that I might wish to find that coach again !"

"You noticed the color of the horses ?"

"Yes, one was white, the other brown or black !"

"Might there not have been a covering on one or the other ?"

"No, I think not—and the driver was an Irishman !"

"That is no clue. Nearly all the hack-drivers in town are Irish, and a saucy, cheating, good for nothing set of scoundrels they are too. If you were to rake the dominions of his sulphuric majesty with a fine-toothed comb, you couldn't find a more un-principled, rascally set ! Have you the cord which you cut off ?"

"I have !" replied the wife, going to her work-basket and producing it from a needle-book, where she had carefully placed it.

"I shall take it to my good friend, Justice M———, and tell him of these facts, and I think, between us, we will soon get on the trace of the poor boy !" said the husband. "If we once find the hack-driver, we can force him to take us to the house of this Genlis, and we'll soon see, then, what his magic is made of !"

" You will not be jealous with me again, Edward ?" asked the young wife, as she looked up fondly in his face.

" No,—my own dear—*dear* Annie! this has been our first quarrel—it shall be our last! But you will own that things looked a little suspicious?" replied he, as he tenderly kissed the high fair brow from which he pushed aside the clustering curls.

" Yes, but I did not know that I talked in my sleep, Edward !"

" Oh! that is an old habit of yours. Often and often have I awakened in the night, and found you clasping me to your bosom, and calling me by every fond name that you could think of, and still you were sound asleep !"

" It is a second nature with me, dearest !" said the blushing wife, " one that will not offend you, I hope !"

" *Offend* me ? My own sweet Annie,—it is my greatest joy. If our poor boy was only restored to our arms, I should be perfectly happy. I am now happier than I was, for I have feared that Willie was dead. Now I am satisfied that he is living, and has only been stolen from us, to extort money !"

" I pray God that we may soon find him. I cannot banish the remembrance of that hard-featured old schoolmaster from my mind !" sighed Mrs. A.

The husband now went forth to find his friend, the Police Justice, so as to take measures for tracing the child. He first thought of letting Mrs. A. make Genlis another visit, and of following the carriage that conveyed her; but fearing that Genlis had spies, who would see that the carriage was followed, and alter its destination, he determined upon first quietly finding the carriage and driver, if possible, unknown to Genlis, whose character he had very accurately conjectured.

CHAPTER XI.

"Do you say you know where my poor cousin is?" asked Lize of Frank Hennock, as soon as they had got outside of Jack Circle's crib.

"I shouldn't wonder if I did!" said Frank knowingly. "She's rather slight—about fifteen or sixteen years old, would be pretty if she wasn't so thin—has blue eyes, light curling hair, and wears a black dress!"

"Yes—yes, you have seen her, where is she!" cried Lize eagerly.

"I've some conditions to arrange before I can afford to tell you!" replied the young man.

"Name them, and be quick!" cried Lize.

"Well, the first one is—the money, you said you'd give a hundred dollars."

"So I will!"

"Well, I don't doubt your honor, but as Paul Clifford used to say, I'd like to see the color of your money, Lize!"

"I hav'n't so much with me, Frank!" said the woman, "but if you must have it—I can get it in five minutes. Charley Cooper or old Jack 'll let me have the brads in a minute!"

"I don't care about the money till I show you the girl," said Frank, "and that can't be to-night!"

"Why not? Look here, younker, you know me, and I'm not to be fooled with!" cried the woman angrily.

"I'm not trying to fool with you, Lize!" said he, shrinking back from before her clenched and threatening hand.

"Then tell me where the girl is!"

"If I do, you'll not try to see her to-night?"

"I don't know about that! Is she safe?" asked Lize.

"Yes," replied the thief, "and in good quarters!"

" Then why can't you tell me where she is ?"

" I will, if you'll promise me the money when you see her, and promise not to let them that you'll find with her know that you ever saw me before !"

" Well, tell me—I'll promise !" cried the woman eagerly.

" Then, she's at my master's !"

" What, the old cove that they were just talking about, in there ?".

" Yes—nobody else !"

" How did she come there ?"

" Why, he picked her up fainting in the street and took her in !"

" God bless him—but, Frank, why can't I see her to-night ?"

" Because I don't think it would be right !   When you do come, you mustn't look as if you knew me, and mind, you mustn't break the old bond and betray the gang !"

" No—no, of course not.   But I'd like to see the poor gal. Didn't she look sick and frightened ?"

" Yes—like Ophelia on the banks of——"

" Oh, curse your poetry, younker ; talk sense to me !   How can I manage to see her ?   How can I explain my finding out she was there ?"

" Tell 'em a watchman told you such a girl went in there— and ask after her name !"

" Well, enough said, I'll do it—and if this is indeed my cousin, I'll give you the hundred to-morrow.   I shall be there early— by the way I've forgotten to ask the street and number !"

Frank gave her this information, and then hurried away, leaving her to leisurely take a patrol down through the Park.

" I must raise that hundred myself to-night !" she muttered as she went along.   " Charley would be cross if I asked him for it, and Jack Circle don't like lending money !"

She walked on, keeping on the shady side of the street, and still soliloquizing :

" I wish I could make one good haul !" she said—" I'd take Angy and go off into the country somewhere.   I want to quit this dreadful life !   I'd run a big risk to do it, and I must make a raise to-night !"

As she made this last remark, she crossed from Centre street into the Park, and assuming her most graceful style, walked slowly down towards that part where the fountain now flings its beautiful jet into the air, when "the powers that be" feel sufficiently liberal to spare the Croton.

The Park was nearly deserted, and Lize walked past the few stragglers there without any success. None of them answered her significant "ahem"—no one followed her, though she lingered along the shadowy paths.

"This won't do," she murmured—"it's a bad season to make a raise here! I must try the Astor once more!"

She hurried across the street, and throwing her veil back from her fine bold features, and drawing her shawl closer around her waist to display her figure, sailed slowly down past the American and Astor hotels. Still, like a badly managed theatre, she failed to draw. Down past the Franklin next she wended her weary way, but in vain did she look for a victim. But she was not one to despair.

" 'Tis a bad night for the Battery," said she, "but I'll try that, too!"

She hurried down there, but it was almost deserted. A few persons were hurrying along the path which led down to Castle Garden, but the other paths were deserted. The wind whistled through the limbs of the leafless trees, the waves came up from the bay with their short and sullen dash against the stone wall, and everything seemed cold, harsh, and uninviting.

Lize glanced upon the bay a moment, slowly passed by the entrance to Castle Garden, and then returned towards Broadway. She was just passing out through the gateway, when she heard a step close behind her, and a feeble voice addressed her :

"For pity's sake, help me, lady! I am a poor old man, who has just been landed from a foreign vessel, and I'm like to freeze to death the first night that I have passed in my native land for fifteen years!"

"There's nothing to be made out of him, at any rate!" muttered the girl, as she turned and glanced at the person who spoke to her. The light of the lamp at the corner fell across the path where he stood, and illuminated his features. There was nothing very peculiar in them; his face was pale, thin, wrinkled, and hollow, but such faces are very common here, and his thin white hairs blew out from beneath the rim of a much worn hat. A mantle covered his form, which seemed to bend with age and weakness, and yet he had not even a staff to lean upon. We said that he looked as hundreds do, who can easily be found in this great city; that there was nothing very strange in his aspect of misery and poverty; yet Lize started back as she looked upon him.

"My God!" she murmured; "can it be *him!*"

Then she took but two long strides to reach his side, and as she looked down upon his face, she cried:

"Who are you—speak; is your name Lindsay—Robert Lindsay?"

"Yes," replied the old man, feebly; "yes, that name was well known in this city once! But who are you that seem to know me?"

"Oh God, my *father*, and in beggary!" groaned Lize.

"Father! beggary!" muttered the old man. "What do you mean, lady?"

"Had you not a daughter once—her name Catharine Lindsay?" asked Lize, eagerly.

"Yes—Kate was a wild, sad girl. She drove me mad, nearly; but she is dead, God forgive her, as I have!"

"No, my father, she is *not* dead!" shrieked the girl: "she lives, and kneels here for you to curse her; she deserves it!" and there, upon the frozen ground, she knelt, while the great tears rushed in torrents down her painted cheeks.

"No, no. You are a tall, handsome woman. My Kate was a darling little girl; it is fifteen years since I saw her, yet I remember her well. But she is dead; I got the letter years ago!"

"It was a false one, I wrote it myself. It was signed by the name of Bradford Kibbey!" cried Lize.

"Yes, that was the name! how did you know that?"

"I wrote that letter myself, father, for you *are* my *father!* I have grown since you fled from your wicked child, grown in stature and in sin! oh God! I wish that I had died; curse me, father, curse me!"

"No!" said the old man, in a trembling tone; "if you are

indeed my Kate, I will bless you. I came here to find your mother's grave, and to lie down upon it, and die !"

"Oh, my father, do not talk of dying ! I will aid you. I have not much money, but it is enough to take care of you !"

"I do believe you are my child, but you're so altered !" said the old man, as he looked up in the face of Lize. Then another thought came into his brain.

"Why were you walking down here ?" he asked.

"I was sick and feverish !" she replied. "I came down here to let the cold wind blow from off the water upon my burning forehead !"

"Are you married, Kate—have you a home ?"

"No," responded Lize, "I am boarding ; but I will take you at once to a lodging-house. You need food and rest. These you shall have, and to-morrow I will provide for you better !"

"Bless you, my girl. God has sent you to me. I might have frozen to death in the streets, if it had not been for you !" said the old man.

"Don't talk that way. Come with me—lean upon my arm— I am strong !" said Lize ; and she hurried her father to one of the little taverns which stood near the water on the North River.

Here, on producing funds, she soon got a comfortable room for him, and some warm supper, which seemed very necessary, for he looked like a living skeleton.

As he gained a little strength, he began to ask Lize questions, but these were so painful to her, and so difficult to respond to, without letting him know her situation, that she determined to leave him as soon as she could. She found that his mind was wandering upon many points : that his reason was much deranged.

She therefore left him money for his immediate use, and bade him remain there quietly till the morrow, when she would return to him.

"Yes,—yes," murmured the old man. "I've but one other place to go to—only one spot which I want to see, and that is the burying-ground,—up town, where I laid your mother, Kate. She was tall—but not so tall as you ; how you have grown !"

Lize did not respond. The mention of her mother's grave,

and the sight of her father in misery now, who once had been rich and happy, was too much for her firmness to bear.

She burst into tears. The old man heard her choking sobs, and taking her hand, said :

"Don't weep now, Kate. I've not spoken of the past—I will not—but I cannot forget the time when you was *so* pretty, and used to have so many beaux ! Ah, that was a long time ago !"

"Curse them—they and my beauty ruined me, and I ruined you !" cried the woman bitterly.

"Did you, though ? I had forgotten !" said the old man, with a dreamy stare. "Well—well ! this is a strange world—but it isn't round, I've been all over it, and it's *flat !*"

His mind was evidently wandering again, but there was some truth in the last part of his remark. The world is decidedly *flat*, and a great part of it quite stale and unprofitable.

Lize could not trust herself to converse longer with her father—therefore, after kissing him, and saying she would be there in the morning, she left him, comfortably situated, at least for that night, and hurried up Broadway.

She seemed to have forgotten the errand she started out on, for she looked neither to the right or left, nor heeded any of those whom she passed. It was getting late, and she had determined to go home, to hide her grief in the solitude of her room, for she had no joy in finding her father. To see him so poor and wretched, to look upon such a wreck, and remember what he *had* been, was indeed torture to her.

She had nearly reached the street where she would turn off to go to her room, when she found herself impeded by a crowd of young men, most of whom seemed to be drunk, for they all were very noisy.

"There's what I call a *high* old g'hal !" said one of the party, as he looked at Lize.

"Don't you know who she is ?" cried another—"it's big Lize of Thomas street !"

"Known everywhere—my God, it is time for me to die !" groaned the unhappy woman.

"Then you'd go where you'd be better known than anywhere else !" cried one of the party, with a coarse laugh.

"Get out of my way, and let me pass along quietly " cried

Lize, seeing that some of the party were determined to stop her.

"Don't yer wish we would!" cried one of the coarsest of the crowd, thrusting himself directly before her.

She only replied by raising him clear of the pavement, and dashing him into the gutter, and attempting to pass on. But the whole party took up the cause of their discomfited comrade, and Lize was in danger of very rough treatment, when a smaller party hurried up the street, and a large, square-shouldered young fellow pushed into the crowd, crying:

"Ello! what 're ye 'bout yere anyhow? what's the muss?"

At this moment he saw the fellow whom Lize had thrown into the gutter, rush up and strike her, with a broken brick, on the head.

Mose, for this was none other than he, sprang at the coward, and felling him with a single blow, he shouted;

"Strike a ghal, would ye!"

Then shouting to his party to come on, he dashed into the whole crowd that had interrupted poor Lize, and in less than a minute all of them who had not run for it, lay stretched upon the pavement.

He then helped Lize up. She had been stunned by the blow which she had received, but was not much injured.

"Make tracks, old ghal!" said Mose, as soon as she was on her feet, "the watch 'll be along here afore soon—they know I'm out on a spree, myself! They wouldn't go for to come for to try to take me up; but they'd jug you if they could!"

"Yes, they 're always down on us poor women!" said Lize—"they're afeard to take men up, but the women must suffer!"

She then started away, as Mose had advised, and soon turned down the street which led to her room. Just as she turned the corner, a person who had been following her at a distance, stepped up to her side and spoke:

"I didn't know but you'd like comp'ny hum to-night—I rayther guessed you mought be lonesome!" said the man, who turned out to be the down-east bhoy, whom Mose called the 'Postle.

"You may turn around and go back then," said Lize scornfully, as she looked at the scrimped pattern of a man who stood before her.

"Well, that's short and sweet, and kinder like givin' a fe₁ɪer the mitten!" grumbled the 'Postle.

Lize paid no attention to his remark, but passed on, while the 'Postle turned around to rejoin his company, muttering as he went:

"There's some tall gals, here in York, sure, but I don't like their manners! They don't understand courtin' like our folks to hum!"

CHAPTER XII.

"WELL, Sir, what do you want of me?" asked Meadows, of Carlton, in a gloomy tone, when he followed the latter, after separating from Whitmore and Livingston.

"Sit down and take a glass of wine, and I'll tell you!" replied Carlton, shutting the door of the room, and pointing to a table upon which wine and glasses had already been placed.

"I have drunk enough!" replied Meadows, as he seated himself.

"Well, I'm confounded dry!" said the other, pouring out some wine and drinking it. He then asked:

"Do you know how Mr. S—— stands with his Bank——has he much cash deposited?"

"Yes," replied Meadows, "he is preparing to make his Spring remittances to Europe!"

"How large a check have you ever known him to draw at once?" continued the gambler.

"Fifty thousand dollars for a single payment!" replied Meadows.

"Then forty thousand now would be safe, eh?"

"What do you mean——a *forgery?*"

"There's no use in calling it by that name!" replied the gambler. "*Manslaughter*, or *homicide*, always sounds more genteel than the coarse and vulgar term, *Murder!* By the way, Charley, how would you like to kill a man?"

"What, Sir! What do you mean?" asked the clerk in an indignant tone.

"Oh, I only asked for information!" replied the gambler carelessly. "But about this other business—this check, I must trouble you to do that up for me!"

"What, to add forgery to my crimes? Carlton, for God's sake do not drive me deeper into the hellish pit!" groaned Meadows.

"You gave me a bond which specified particularly that you were to *obey* me !" said Carlton, in a deliberate tone, taking a second glass of wine. " You've got your hand in, and you might as well go ahead !"

"Suppose I refuse !"

"Then your little item of *stealing* might be recorded in Court, and an officer request the pleasure of furnishing you with free board at the Tombs !"

"You forget, that no theft can be proved upon me ! The money is paid back——and is safe in the vaults of Mr. S—— !" replied Meadows, with a triumphant smile. "I'm not quite so much in your power as you thought, Mr. Carlton !"

"Indeed !" said the gambler. " Then you mean to have things your own way, eh ?"

"Yes—if you try to force me to go on and intend to make me a slave to your will !"

"You will not fulfil your bond, eh ?"

" No !"

"Why did you sign it ?"

"To get the money back which you had stolen from me at your infernal faro bank !"

"Indeed—that was your reason, eh ! But why did you sign ae confession of having stolen the precise sum of seventeen thousand, eight hundred and fifty dollars !"

" Because I was desperate—you had me in your power *then !*"

"Yes, and I *still* have you in my power," replied the gambler with a sneer. " You have kindly furnished me with the means of recovering that money this very night, if I chose—keys are made by this time to fit the vaults, aye, and every door in your employer's store. I think I could make a very good spec by picking out some of his thousand dollar shawls, some of his hundred dollar handkerchiefs, &c. Our up-town ladies would give a little more than half-price if they were told they were smuggled, eh ?"

" You could not harm me by robbing him in that way. My accounts are all correct !" replied the clerk.

" No—but I think, after all, that the confession and bond might be copied into the Herald—I think some proof might be found, to connect the name of Charles Meadows with robbery. What

an item it would make for Bennett. 'Stupendous villany'—
'confidential clerk'—'weeping mother and distracted sister'—
'accomplished and beautiful girl'—'heartless wretch'—and all
that!" said Carlton, with his customary sneer; and then, as he
saw the effect which his remarks had upon Meadows, he added:

"I happen to have a still stronger hold upon you. Every
bill that I gave you was a counterfeit. They were very good
ones though, and such as I knew would not easily be detected—but a note to Mr. S. connecting your name with a counterfeiting gang, might possibly remove the good impression that
he has of you, especially when he found so much bad money in
hand."

"Oh God—I am indeed in your power!" moaned the clerk.
"And now my ruin is certain—for the money will be refused when
I go to deposit it!"

"Certainly!" replied Carlton—" but you will have things your
own way."

"No—no, do as you wish with me!" groaned Meadows—
"I am indeed your slave!"

"Now you talk sense!" replied the gambler, "and we can
proceed to business! First, I wish you to draw a check for forty thousand in the name of S———. Have it ready for presentation whenever I say the word, leaving the date vacant. Then
make drafts also with his signature on such Southern houses as
you can get cashed here without difficulty. In that way we
can raise sixty or seventy thousand, and on the night of the day
you make this raise, some friends of mine will avail themselves
of your kindness and pay a visit to the vaults and store-room of
your employer's establishment."

"My God!—what a deep planning villain you are!" said the
clerk, in astonishment.

"Rather apt—but it is my trade!" replied the gambler drily.

"How much of all this am I to have?" asked Meadows;
"you know that I must leave before it is found out!"

"Yes, and if all succeeds, I think twenty-five thousand dollars would do for your share!"

"Less than half!"

"Yes—and you have less than half the trouble. The poor
burglars run more risk than you!"

"More risk! Do not I lose all that is worth having—a good name and fair reputation? I tell you plainly—Henry Carlton, if I could recall my first mis-step—the first thought that induced me to take money from my employer to win more with—I would cut off my right hand before I'd pass the portals of a gambling house; yes, I'd cut my throat, rather than do what I have done!"

"Indeed!" said the gambler, with a sneer. "You must be fond of committing suicide! you tried it once here, but made a botch of it!"

"Yes, thank God; it would have ruined my family if I had succeeded!" replied the clerk.

"Well now, we'll drop that, and talk of business again!" said Carlton. "Cheer up and take a glass of wine!"

Meadows took the wine, but he was neither in a mood nor situation to cheer up.

"We must arrange for your escape after the check and drafts are presented!" said Carlton, "I should be as glad to have you safe out of the country then, as you would be yourself!"

"I do not doubt it—if I was taken up I should convict you too!"

"Not at all. There will not be the slightest proof of my connexion with you. You can prove that you gambled at my table *perhaps*, and perhaps you cannot, for men wouldn't like to swear they'd seen you play there, for fear the world, the immaculate and suspicious 'world' would want to know what they were doing there themselves!"

"Where can I go to, what country is the most safe?" asked Meadows.

"Why, as to safety—I think Greenland or Africa would be the best, for they're the only countries where I've never heard of the police!"

"This is not a subject to joke upon!—where can I go and not be followed, and more than that, where can I go and find no accounts of my leaving in the papers? My mother and sister would die of shame if they were to find it out!"

"Cuba. Some of the interior villages of Cuba I think would do. Their government prohibits American papers because they're afraid of our democratic principles!"

"It would be too near!" replied Meadows. "I should be surely recognised at some time!"

"So you would be, if you went to the North Pole, perhaps. There never was but one place where a Yankee did not find his way, yet!".

"And that ———— ?"

"Was Captain Symmes' Hole, and there's no doubt in my mind, but some of the Yankee passengers on board the President are trying to get there now—that is, if she stuck in an ice-island as the mesmerists say!"

Meadows did not heed Carlton's attempt to be witty, but again asked:

"Why could I not go to Buenos Ayres, or Brazil?"

"You're too honest to thrive in those countries. An honest Yankee there would be kicked out of society!"

"Don't torment me with your jokes, Mr. Carlton; they're untimely, to say the least!"

"So they are, my boy, but I wanted to get you in good humor, for I've another piece of business in store for you!"

"What, more villany?"

"No, not exactly *villany*, but a little piece of *justice* on my own private account, which I'll give you five thousand for. That'll swell your purse to thirty thousand, and if you'll go into the interior of Cuba, change your name and buy a plantation, you'll do well!"

"My mother and sister must find all out, if I change my name!"

"So they would, if they found you possessed of so much money, if you didn't have some good excuse!"

"What excuse could I have?"

"Why, tell them you caught old S———— in smuggling, and that the government found out you were a witness, and that he gave you this money and hired you to leave, rather than to stay, and be forced to appear against him!"

"Yes, that would do. But it will require a great deal of management to get off!"

"Leave that to me. Now take another glass of wine, and we'll arrange the other little matter of which I spoke!"

"What is it?" asked Meadows, declining to take more wine.

" As I said before, it's only a small matter.   I have an enemy, a man who has injured me deeply—I want him punished !"

" I am no fighter !" replied Meadows; " you can surely settle your own quarrels !"

" Unfortunately, in this case I cannot, without laying myself too much under suspicion.   It is known that I am the man's sworn and deadly foe—while you do not even know him, and of course would not be suspected !"

" But why so much fear of the law ?   Surely if a man injures you and you thrash him, the law will do no more than fine you a few dollars !"

" That is true; but, in this case, my man must get more than a thrashing !"

" What do you mean ?"

" Only that he must get a few inches of steel through his heart, or a bullet through his brain !"

Meadows shrank back in horror from the cold-blooded villain.

" What !" he gasped ; " do you expect me to commit a murder for you ?"

" Certainly, if I wish it done ; the bond specified obedience to *all* my demands !"

" But not *murder ;* oh God ! spare me from that !"

" Sorry I can't make it convenient to excuse you, but the fact is, you're the only *friend* I have that I can use !"

" Where is Selden ?   He was made for an assassin, you can see it in his eye.   You know that he has courage ; he has already stabbed his man !"

" Yes, and he is too well known for me to use him in this case.   I choose you, because you are unknown, and no one will suspect you !"

" Oh God ! I cannot do that, Carlton.   Anything else, but spare me from that ! I would not have strength to strike a blow !" groaned Meadows.

" It requires very little strength to pull a trigger," replied the gambler, " and I shall have everything so prepared in this case, that there will be no danger to you whatever."

" Who is the man ?"

"I cannot tell you that; it is enough that you do not know him!"

"But if I do not know him, how can I do what you wish?"

"That shall all be arranged. He shall be brought to you, you shall have neither difficulty nor danger to encounter!"

"I cannot, dare not do it!" murmured Meadows.

"You can, and must!" replied Carlton. "I will have no trifling in this matter. You are in my power, and *must* do as I wish! When this is done, and our raise made out of old S——, you shall have no more trouble, but shall be placed on board a vessel bound to Cuba—you, and your mother and sister! I'll pledge my *honor* for that!"

His *honor*—the honor of a professional blackleg! Let the devil talk of his *religion* after that; or a beggar of his wealth; or a prostitute of her virtue!

Meadows sighed, as he paused to think of the dreadful proposition of Carlton. He was, indeed, in a dilemma. Certain ruin was his, if he dared to persist in a refusal, for the gambler had him in his power; and if he consented, he might safely leave the country with his mother and sister, possessing sufficient fortune to make them comfortable for life in a foreign land. He did not pause to think how easy and natural it would be for the gambler to break his word to him after all the villany had been finished; he was in the net, and was blind to everything save his own immediate danger.

"I will leave you to think of this matter until to-morrow!" said Carlton; "I *know* you'll be secret on the subject!"

"Yes, yes; but do spare me from the murder!"

"Pshaw! man, call it homicide—*justifiable* homicide, and it wont look half so bad to you!"

"How can it be justifiable?" asked the clerk.

"Because this man has done me the deepest wrong on earth!" replied the gambler, in a deep tone, while his eye flashed with the memory of the wrong. "He has seduced the wife of my bosom—the only being on earth that I *love*, except the children she has borne me! He has torn her heart from me—he has stained her with a black and damning shadow that not even his blood can wash away!"

Meadows shuddered as he looked upon the now flushed face

of the gambler, and saw the fearful working of the storm of passion, which he had restrained all this time.

"I would kill him myself," he continued, "but I will at any rate be suspected and arrested. I'll have to prove an alibi! Sam Selden 'll have to do the same! There is but one other that could do it, and I'm afraid to trust *her* hand!"

"Mine would be a weak one, I fear!" said Meadows.

"You love your sister?" said Carlton.

"Yes—I do, as few brothers can!"

"Were she seduced—blasted—ruined, would you have a weak hand if you stood armed before her seducer?" cried Carlton.

"No—I would cleave his heart were it guarded with a coat of mail!" said Meadows.

"Then strike but one blow for me—and you shall have the power to make your mother and sister happy for ever! Meadows, I have talked harshly to you—have threatened you and all that—but do this one favor for me—I ask it as a favor—and I will be the best friend you ever had. I will give you fifty thousand dollars; yes, for his heart's blood I'd almost give his weight in gold—you will do it, won't you?"

Carlton, in his excitement, had forgotten the bond, forgotten that he was the master. His usual pallor had deserted him, and his eyes gleamed like sparks of living fire.

Meadows filled a glass with wine—dashed it down his throat, and in a low husky whisper asked:

"When must it be done?"

"Soon, *very* soon. I'll let you know to-morrow!"

"Give me till then to decide!"

"No—now—*now!*" cried the gambler—"I must have all uncertainty off my mind! I shall go mad, and be fool enough to murder him myself. Speak, will you do it?"

"My hand would tremble, I could never reach his heart with the steel!"

"A pistol shall be your weapon!"

"Its report would bring aid to him—I shall be detected!"

"No—I have arranged everything for that in my mind already, and walked over the spot where he must die—and have seen the course which you must take. I had but just come from there when I met you—and had just seen him—the wretch who must die! You need not fear—I pledge you my sacred honor, that for you there is not the slightest danger. You never will be suspected. I'll prepare the weapon myself, and I'll take good care that it shall not be loaded to *snap* this time!"

"I'll see you to-morrow!" said Meadows gloomily—again swallowing some wine.

"Well—let it be so, you'll do it for me, Charley!"

"I suppose I *must!* I'm your slave!" replied the clerk.

"No—rather say my FRIEND if you'll do me this favor!" replied Carlton.

After taking some more wine, they separated—Meadows to return to his mother's house.—Carlton to repair to his faro table, and meet some of the *respectable* citizens of this great city.

CHAPTER XIII.

POOR Angelina! A second day of sickness had dawned upon her, and though she looked far more beautiful than she had on the night before, her very beauty indicated the fearful progress of her disease. Her cheeks were flushed and of a rosy hue; her blue eyes seemed larger and brighter than ever. Yet the blue veins on her throbbing temples were dark and swollen— her pale lips quivered, and every now and then opened with a low moan of suffering, while her frame was convulsed with the racking pain of the fever.

Mr. Precise had not closed his eyes all night. He had given his bed up to Jenny, though the latter had offered to sit up and watch with the invalid. So far as being sleepless, he had not had the advantage of the sick girl. She had not slept—but had lain and tossed with pain, all the night.

"I am so glad it is day once more!" she murmured, as the grey light of early dawn came in through the open shutters of the window.

"Yes—you've had a hard night—poor creetur!" said Mr. Precise, kindly—" but never mind, the doctor 'll be here soon, and 'll cure you up."

" No—no!" sighed the girl, " you are taking all this trouble for nothing. I feel as if I should not get well!"

"Don't talk that way! you'll soon be well and hearty as a spring lamb!" said the old gentleman, while a tear came up in either eye. "Turn over and try to sleep, child—I'll have some gruel made for you, agin the time you wake up!"

" I will try," murmured the sufferer—" but my eyes ache as if they were coming out. My head seems as if it was all on fire!"

"Poor creetur! I wish I could bear it all for you!" said the old gentleman.

"Oh! God bless you, sir, you are too kind to me!" replied the sufferer.

"No, my child, no indeed! we can never be too kind to the suffering whom we meet. But go to sleep now—that's a good girl! I'll not talk to you any more!"

The old gentleman leaned back in his easy chair as he said this, but he did not keep silent very long, though he said no more, for he almost instantly dropped into a slumber himself, and began to snore very loudly. His snoring, too, was almost like talking. First it would come out with a long, low, swelling murmur, with a gradual rise in the intonation, as if he was asking a question. Then would come a short, quick snort, like a cross single-syllabled answer! Then, again, his nasal member would seem to imagine itself a stage horn, for it would give a very good imitation of that instrument, we mean of the small straight tin horn, used by western stage-drivers.

Angelina lay there and listened to this singular music for some time, until Jenny came into the room. As she did so, Mr. Precise woke.

"Well, I do declare! Why, I must have gone to sleep!" he muttered, as he rubbed his eyes. "What time is it, Jenny?"

"Breakfast-time, sir!" replied the girl. "The muffin-man has been here—and I've got your coffee ready!"

"Make some gruel for this poor girl,—why, my dear, haven't you been to sleep yet?"

"No, sir, I am not sleepy!" murmured the sufferer.

"Well,—it was so strange that I should go to sleep, and then, I had a dream, too!"

"A dream, sir?" repeated Angelina, wondering what he could have dreamed about while he snored so loud.

"Yes, and it was such a strange one. It was about my new plan for the good of the poor. I thought that I was on the farm that I'm going to have laid out for them—and that the houses were all built, and the fields laid out, and the people all at work, and I stood there looking at them and rubbing my hands with joy, when all of a sudden, I heard a loud noise like a gun fired, or a peal of thunder, and everything sank out of my sight. While I stood there, wondering what on earth all this meant, I **thought I saw an angel stand before me, dressed all in white,** with great white wings, and a face just like yours, my dear, and it looked very mournfully at me, and shook its head sadly three times. I was just going to speak to it, when it flew away up into the sky,—and then I woke up!"

"Wall,—I never!" cried Jenny, who, with mouth and eyes wide open, had been listening.

"Go and make the gruel, Jenny!" said Mr. Precise, sharply; then, as he turned and looked at Angelina, he saw that tears were stealing down her cheeks.

"Do you believe in dreams, my dear?" he asked.

"Yours will come true, sir!" she replied,—"I know I shall die very soon!"

"Oh! God forbid," said the old gentleman fervently,—"it would be too hard for you to die now, when your troubles are all over!"

"There's a woman down stairs—a great tall woman, who wants to know if there aint no such girl here as Angelina Lindsay!" said Jenny, who had just come up stairs.

"That's my name—it must be my cousin!" murmured Angelina.

"What shall I do—shall I let her come up?—she looks awful fierce!" said the maid.

"I'll go and see who she is!" replied Mr. Precise, "but, Jenny, haven't you got this poor girl's gruel ready yet? I do declare you're as slow as a new 'prentice!"

"I'll have it up in a minute, sir!"

Mr. Precise went down stairs, and soon returned with the visitor, who, of course, was Lize.

The woman saw Angelina, and rushing to her bedside covered her feverish cheeks with kisses, while tears of mingled joy and sorrow gushed from her eyes.

"Oh! God, my poor, poor gal—I've been e'en a'most crazy about you—why did you run away from the boardin'-house?"

"I saw *him*—that young man who has tormented me so. He came to the house after me!" replied Angelina.

"There,—it was just what I thought! You saw him and ran away—he didn't know you was there. He was there to see some one else—but you're sick. Your head is hot as fire!"

"Yes, cousin Eliza, I am sick!"

"Don't call me Eliza, dear, poor Angy, any more. My real name is Kate, Kate Lindsay, *you* must never call me by any other. There is but one in this town besides you now, that knows my real name!"

"Who is that?" asked the invalid.

"My father—your uncle, Angy!"

"Why, cousin, you never told me this before! I would like to see my uncle before I die—where is he?"

"Down town—I found him last night—a poor beggar in the streets. He had just landed from over the seas. He was a beggar, and it has been all my fault!" groaned the unhappy woman.

"He shall have a home on my ' Poor Farm!' " said Mr. Precise, who, seeing Lize weep, could not keep his own eyes free from salt water.

"Can he not come here to see me?" asked Angelina—"I am too weak to walk—but I would so like to see him before I die!"

"Before you *die!*" echoed Lize—"Oh, God, she is not so sick as *that*, is she!"

Then turning to Mr. Precise, she asked,

"Do, pray tell me, sir, if she is in danger!"

Mr. Precise could not answer.

"She is—she *is!*" shrieked the woman, "and it's all my fault; I ought never to have left her side. Oh, God, why is everything that I love, cursed and blasted!"

"Don't fret, dear cousin, it is not your fault, and this gentleman has been so very kind to me!"

"Oh, God bless him for it—he never shall be the loser—but!"

A thought came like lightning over the mind of poor Lize, she remembered that this was the master of Frank Hennock—that he was the very man whom her gang was trying to rob.

"It shall not be!" she muttered. "No—No—he shall not suffer, if I have to blab it all out!"

"What does she mean!" said Mr. Precise—noticing the wild looks and strange language of the woman. "What do you mean, my good woman?"

"To save you from harm—beware of ————, hush, I'll tell you some other time!" said Lize, pausing in an instant, as the door opened, and Frank Hennock made his appearance.

"I'm ready to attend to that business for you, sir!" said the young rascal, looking as composedly as if he had never seen Lize before.

"Very well, Francis, go down to the parlor—I'll try and come down directly!"

"How is the poor young lady, sir?" asked Frank, who, noticing the agitation of Lize, began to think it was not best to leave her alone with Mr. Precise.

"Sick—very sick," replied Mr. Precise.

"The doctor's here, sir!" said Jenny, popping her head into the room, "and the gruel's ready, Sir!"

"I must go for a little while—I promised to see my father this morning!" said Lize, "but I'll be back afore night, and if you please, sir, I'll watch with my cousin till she is better!"

"Yes—poor thing, you may. You're a good woman to think so much of her, poor creetur, but she sha'n't suffer while you're gone!"

The doctor entered at this moment, and as he took the hand of his patient, and glanced at her face, a shadow of care and pain came over his countenance.

Lize watched him closely as if she would read the fate of her cousin in his look, and tears gushed from her eyes, when she saw his look of anxiety.

"Save her, doctor, save her life, and I'll give you all the money I can raise!"

The doctor smiled, and replied:

"We'll do our best for her; but money would not add to my skill. We will hope for the best!"

Lize turned away to hide the scalding tears which rushed down her cheeks, which were very pale now. She had taken no time to put paint upon them that morning.

"I'll go, now," said she, "and I'll be back the earlier!' Good by, Angy! God bless you!" and she kissed the sick girl fervently.

Frank Hennock followed her down stairs, apparently to let her out at the front door, but really to get a chance to speak to her.

"Lize," said he, as he stood at the door step, "you're not **going to 'blow' on us to the old man?**"

"No, Frank, but you've got to stop robbing him. He's acted like a livin' angel to that poor gal, and I'll not see him harmed ! you've got to stop short where you are, or I *will* blow, that's sure as gospel !"

"You know what a risk you'd run in doing it, don't you !"

"Yes, and you'd run the risk of 'commodations up the river for a while, too !" replied the woman.

"Well, but you'll go and see old Jack, and get him to agree to it, wont you ?" asked Frank.

"Yes, and I'll make him pay the old man his money on the forged check, too !" said Lize; "he shan't suffer by any of our gang, when he's acted so kind to my cousin as all this comes to. You've had enough, and too much out of him a'ready !"

"Well, just fix it with old Jack, and I'm easily satisfied. I kinder like the old covey, myself !" replied Frank. And then he added :

"You've not forgotten the hundred dollars, have you, Lize ?"

"No, but I've not had time to raise it yet !" replied Lize; "I'll get it of Charley Cooper to-day for you. I'm going to live on the square after this, Frank !"

"What ! and desert *us*, your old comrades and companions in war ?"

"I shall never go on the cross again !"

"Then, farewell to all your greatness ! why, Lize, I thought you'd more ambition !"

"Not in that line," replied Lize; "but I must go. Remember, now, the old gentleman is not to suffer any more !"

"Of course not, of course not, if *you* say so, Miss Eliza !" and Frank bowed low, and gallantly kissed his hand, as the tall woman hurried away.

Then he muttered to himself :

"This treason must be nipped i' the bud ! as Shakspeare says. We'll have to clap a stopper on her jaw-tackle, or she'll blow the gaff ! as Cooper says in the Water-Witch !"

"What witch ? was that great tall woman a witch ?" asked Jenny, who had just come up stairs to inform Frank that his breakfast was ready.

"She looked a little like one, didn't she !" laughed Frank.

"Well, she was a strange lookin' creetur; but what was you

a sayin' so petikler like?" asked Jenny, a little disposed to be jealous.

"Oh, nothing, only speaking of the sick girl up stairs, who, it appears, is her cousin!"

"I wish she'd kept her cousin to hum, so I do!" replied Jenny, spitefully; "our master's taken such a likin' to her, that there's no doin' anythin' with him now. I'd been expectin' all the time that he'd do sumthin' for us when we got married, and now, I do believe he's goin' to 'dopt her, and call her Miss Precise!"

"Shouldn't wonder if he did!" replied Frank.

"Then he'll do nuthin' for us when we get married!"

"Oh, yes, I'm sure he will, *when* we do!" replied Frank; "but talking of that, let's go down to breakfast!"

———

After leaving the house of Mr. Precise, Lize, or Kate Lindsay, as she really should be called, hurried down to the lodging-house where she had left her father the night before.

Upon her asking for him, to her terror and surprise, the landlord told her he had gone out a few minutes after she had left, on the night before. He could not tell her which way the poor old man had gone, but said that he seemed quite smart after eating and drinking, and talked very lively, and said he was going to see his wife.

"His wife!" cried Lize, "she's been dead nearly twenty years. Oh God! he must be crazy. I thought he talked very strange!"

Then the thought struck her that he might have wandered off towards the graveyard where her mother had been buried, and she determined to seek him there. Leaving directions with the landlord to detain him, if he returned, till she could see him, the woman turned her steps sadly in the direction which she supposed he might have taken. She was very wretched. Everything seemed to work wrong with her. Those in whom she took any interest seemed to suffer, as if for her sins. Poor

Angelina, she feared, was on her death-bed, and now she trembled for her weak and unhappy father, for it had been a cold and frosty night.

30

CHAPTER XIV

Frank Hennock went up stairs to his master as soon as he had finished his breakfast, for he felt uneasy lest Lize might have dropped some hint about her knowledge of him or his character.

The doctor had gone, and Angelina had sunk into a fitful slumber, or rather doze, for ever and anon she would start and mutter in incoherent language, as if terrible dreams were raving through her burning brain.

Mr. Precise laid his finger on his lip, as Frank entered, for him to keep silent, and the latter went in on tip-toe. Bending his lips close to Mr. Precise's ear, he whispered:

" Wont you go down and eat, sir, I'll stay here and watch her !"

" No, Francis, you're a good boy to think of me, but I can't eat now. I'm afraid that poor creetur is agoin to die !" and the old man took out his handkerchief, not to hide his tears, but to wipe them away.

Frank sighed, and put his handkerchief up to his face too, and said :

" Oh, sir, I hope not. She is so beautiful and looks so good !"

" She bears her suffering like an angel, she does !" said the old man, " and the poor creetur has only seen the dark side o life. I want her to live and enjoy the sunshine a little while. If she dies I shall never be happy agin !" and a broken sob burst from his lips.

" What a strange woman that cousin of hers seemed to be !" said Frank.

" Yes, and I'd forgotten, but she talked very strangely to me. I must see her again and get an explanation !"

" What did she say ?" asked Frank, tremulously.

" Water—just a drop, if you please !" murmured the invalid,

"I am so hot. Oh, mercy—my head will burst open with this dreadful pain !"

Mr. Precise sprang to help the poor girl, and Frank could not get the explanation which he desired, but his own guilt made him picture it ten times worse than it really was, and as soon as he could do so, he begged Mr. P.'s permission to be absent for a little while—saying that he wanted to see his sick mother. He readily gained this permission, for Mr. Precise cared little about attending to business just then. He was not a man who *could* think of many things at once, and his whole heart and soul had become interested in the fate of the poor sewing-girl.

Frank hurried, therefore, as soon as possible, to the house of Jack Circle. He found the latter in his little front bar-room attending to his usual business, but as he passed through into the back-room, he gave him a sign, and Jack soon followed him.

"What's hup now ?" asked old Jack, "what brings you here in the day time ?"

"Treason ! Clouds dark and ominous hang o'er our house !" cried Frank, assuming a tragical air.

"Clouds be d——d !" said old Circle, who had no ear for poetry—"What's the row ? Talk plain hinglish to me—I don't hunderstand nuthin else !"

"Well then—to descend to the grade of your understanding, *we* are in danger !" said Frank.

"'Ow ?" cried old Jack, "'as any one blowed the gaff ?"

"No—not yet, that I know of, but still I have my fears, as George Washington Dixon said about the revolution in Yucatan !"

"Oh, blast your Dixons and revolutions—just speak hout and let hus know what's hup ?"

"Well, you know big Lize !"

"Don't know nobody else, she's a reg'lar gallows gal, she is !" replied old Jack.

"May be yes, and may be no !" replied Frank. "She's gettin' offish lately, and I'm afeared she'll blow the gaff !"

"*She !*" cried Jack in surprise. "Why, she's one of the best ands in the whole gang ! No, you needn't be afeared o' her !"

"But she is the one I am afeared of—she saw my master this morning."

"Wh—what !" cried Circle—"not to blow on us ?"

"No—but, you see, he picked up the girl she was asking after the other night—and she's Lize's cousin, and Lize feels grateful, and she don't want us to *do* the old man!"

"Well, that's kind o' nateral, too, in Lize!" said old Jack, "but it wont do for us! We've laid out to lift all we can, and 'elp your gov'nor to take care of his property, and she musn't go for to hinterfere!"

"How will you stop it? She has already said something to put him on his guard, I expect!"

"The bloody 'ell, she has!" cried Jack—"we must jug her, till arter we've cracked his crib! She didn't say nuthin habout the check?"

"No, I think not—but she's to see again him this afternoon!"

"No she wont!" replied Jack, "not if she can be found afore that. I've got a snug berth down in the cellar, for sich as she! Blow the gaff? Why blast her heyes, she's forgotten the rules. I'll have her 'unted up—she'll be here to see me on petikler bizness, afore she's three hours older!"

"That 'll be the only way to keep all safe!" said Frank.

"Yes—but I'm not one as can be kotched napping any 'ow!" said Jack. "I'll fix the lady, I will! Come hout and take summat vet; a pot o' yale, or some 'alf-and-'alf!"

Frank complied with the invitation, and then hastened to return to his master.

"Hit's werry hodd," soliloquized Jack after Frank had gone away—"hit's werry hodd in Lize to take sich a kink inter 'er 'ead! But there's no tellin' what a 'ooman won't do, if she takes a likin' to a creetur! I thought Lize was safe as a lost ha'penny—but she was allers a wilful human, and there's no more dependin' on a wilful 'ooman, than on a skeery cracksman!"

The old man's daughter Harriet came in at this moment.

"Where've you been, 'Arriet my gal?" asked Jack.

"Round to Jew Mikes—to get the tin for them spoons!" replied she.

"'Ow much did he give—is he goin' to melt 'em?"

"No. He give me the same he did afore! He's agoin' to scrape off the name—rub 'em down and put 'em up for new in the Broadway crib!"

"He's keen, even for a sheeney!" replied Jack, but his conversation was interrupted at this moment by the entrance of customers.

CHAPTER XV.

WHEN poor Isabella Meadows came to herself, she found that she was in a small room, well furnished, but hung around with licentious and obscene pictures. She shuddered as she judged the character of the place from this; but she felt some relief, on finding herself alone. She arose from the couch whereon she had been carelessly thrown, and going to the door, tried the lock. It had been fastened outside. She glanced around the room, and saw that there was a window in front. She quickly tried the shutters of that, and found that they, too, had been fastened—apparently nailed from the outside.

"No hope, not even the means of death!" she murmured.

She looked at the small toilette table where the single light burned, which illuminated the small, close room. Several books were upon it. She glanced at them, and read the titles:— "Ernest Maltravers," "The Mysteries of Paris," "Byron's Works," "Moore's Poetry," "Tom Jones," "Charlotte Temple," were the titles she looked at, but, at last—strange place and company for such a book, she found a BIBLE! She looked at it —a small, handsomely gilt copy; and turning over the first leaves, her eyes met the owner's name, written thus on a blank leaf;

"Presented to *Gertrude*, by her affectionate mother!"

Who was Gertrude—where was she, and the "affectionate mother" who had given her that precious volume which alone should have kept her from that house and its miserable practices? Alas! what might she have been, when that Bible was given her—what might she be now! What pictures could the imagination paint, what contrasts could it form; the transition from comfort, from the smiles of fond and idolizing parents, from the purity of stainless maidenhood, to the hell of that atmosphere, to the life of the painted, heart-broken courtesan, whose smile is like sun-light falling upon a tomb. There may be brightness without, yet *within*, there is wretchedness and misery; darker, colder, more bitter than death!

I do not, with all the world, condemn, upbraid, and curse the poor, hapless courtesans of the town. I *pity* more than I condemn, for two-thirds of them are driven to that life by the perfidy of men, and not by their own evil passions; for woman, frail woman, was ever but too weak and confiding, man by nature but too deceptive. And the world, with its sneers and frowns, bars all return to a virtuous life, if once a poor woman passes the bounds of maidenly propriety. A man may sin and sin again, and still be *respectable*, his virtue is seldom questioned; but let a woman make one mis-step, and her fame is blasted for ever: she is an outcast from society, she is a spotted thing, which not even death can purify. So, from their actions, seem to think the people of this world; so cannot we think, for it is indeed a poor rule which will not work both ways. It is, indeed, a poor rule which will for ever blast a woman's fame, if she yield to the persuasions of a seductive man; and, at the same time, let the man pass scot-free from censure, or, at least, but feel the breath of condemnation, as the reed which for a moment bends to the passing gale, and then rises upright as before. We condemn immorality in all cases; but we will not, in our condemnation, distinguish between the sexes, except to look with more severity upon the immoralities of the stronger sex; for they, being looked up to by the fairer and weaker sex, should ever be their protectors and guardians, instead of their enemies and destroyers.

But, dropping this moralizing paragraph, we will return to our story.

When Isabella took up the Holy Book, and glanced at the writing, she burst into tears. The memory of her own fond mother and her idolized brother came across her mind. Little did they dream of her misery and peril.

She trembled as she heard the bolt of her door turned back, for she expected to see the hated form of Whitmore, and her heart was full of terror. But she was pleasantly disappointed. A young and very pretty girl entered, and then Isabella heard the door locked again by some one who was outside.

"I have come to stay with you to-night!" said the girl. "Mrs. Swett said you might be lonesome, or feel bad, and want company!"

"Then *he* has gone away?" said Isabella.

"If you mean your beau, I s'pose he has, or the old woman wouldn't have sent me up here, 'specially as the parlor was full of company!"

"I'm glad he is not here—but why am I kept here—why was the door locked just now?"

"Oh! they always do that when a girl first comes here, till she gets a little used to the place! They kept me locked in a whole month, before they'd even let me go down in the parlor!"

"Then you did not come here willingly?"

"Oh! no, indeed! I came to town from ———, up the river, to get work—or to get into a milliner's. When I got down in the boat, I asked a hackman to take me to a respectable boarding-house, and he brought me here! I don't like to tell you the rest—but I've been here six months now! I was very unhappy for a while, but I'm used to it now!"

"Poor girl!" said Isabella, for the moment forgetting her own perilous situation, "had you no friends?"

"Yes, a mother and two sisters, but Ma'am S. wouldn't let me write to them, and now, I suppose, they think I'm dead!"

"But don't you want to escape from here?"

"No,—not now. What would be the use—I'm ruined for everything but this!" replied the girl. "No one would give me work—I could not get a place anywhere, it is my only chance for a decent living to stay here now! I get clothes and all I want to eat, and when I get melancholy, I drink wine till I get happy, and forget everything!"

"Oh, God!—is it possible that such a life can be led?" moaned Isabella.

"Oh! you'll get used to it!" said the girl. "I used to talk and fret, but I found it was of no use, so I made the best of a bad bargain!"

"Who is Gertrude, I saw her name in a book on the table?" asked Isabella.

"Oh! she *was* a very pretty girl. She belonged up town somewhere; her beau promised to marry her, and got her here in that way. She took on very hard, because he left her after a month or so, and got very sick. Ma'am S. took her up town to her other house, and she never came back again. I heard she'd died, and I asked her beau about it, but he said he didn't know, nor care. That is all I know of her—only I've heard her parents were very rich, and that her father drove a carriage, and lived in a big house up town! She never would talk to us girls, but used to sit up here, and cry all the time nearly!

"She wouldn't go down in the parlor to see company, and Ma'am S. would curse her for it, and wouldn't send her up anything to eat for a day at a time!"

"Poor creature—and must my fate be hers!" murmured Isabella.

"Why, you're not agoin' to be a fool, and stand out agin the old woman and your beau, are you?" asked the girl in reply.

"Yes—I will die before I will submit to anything wrong!" replied Isabella. "Will you not help me to get away from them?"

"I dare not—the old woman would never forgive me!" replied the girl.

"Oh, God have mercy on me!" moaned Isabella—"why am I left to such a horrible fate! I wish I could die this night!"

"I often wish so!" said the girl, "but then I drink and get merry and forget how bad I am! If I was to keep sober all the time, and let myself think of home and my mother, I'd go crazy!"

"Is there no way to get out of this horrible house? I know but too well what it is!"

"No—Ma'am S. always keeps the key and lets every one in and out. They say she's very rich, but she don't act so with us poor girls. She manages to get all we make—but if you like, let's go to bed. It's getting late and I'd like to sleep to-night. I've had to keep up late every night, and I do feel as if a good night's rest would be so good!"

"You can sleep if you like"—said Isabella, "but for me, I cannot. Oh, is there not some way of getting out of here?"

"If you had plenty of money you might—the old woman would do anything for money !"

"Alas !" sighed Isabella, " I have none ! Would to God that I had the means of ending my life !"

Poor girl—her prospect was indeed dark. Her companion soon retired, and glad of a chance to rest, soon fell into a sound slumber. But Isabella could not close her eyes. She could hear the sound of laughter and revelry below—and she shuddered at every sound, for she feared, more than all, the return of Whitmore. She did not dream of submitting to the fate which had befallen the poor girl, who slept before her—she determined rather to die. And yet how many cases are there in this city, precisely similar to that which she had just heard! There are *thousands !* This is no fiction, reader—*indeed* it is not! From many a quivering lip I have heard just such a tale, while scalding tears have fallen from weary eyes ; I have listened to many a moan from a heart well nigh broken ; I have heard the wretched wish for death to come and end their miseries.

And these are they who *can* be reformed—who would bless the hand which would draw them forth from the vortex of wretchedness and infamy wherein they have fallen, but who are thrust back, if they try to escape, by a harsh, unpitying, hypocritical world.

If there is one class in this city which more deserves our pity and aid than another, it is this—and there is no field half so extensive before the philanthropist.

There are at the very least *fifteen thousand* of these wretched creatures in this city—counting up the white and black, and of these probably *five* thousand are poor country girls, who did, not enter willingly into the life they lead—but came here poor, yet innocent, and have been *forced* into their present misery through ignorance or helplessness.

When the writer was gathering notes for this work, one year ago, he came across the unhappy girl who is introduced in the above scene, and when he asked her why she did not leave the horrible life she was leading, her tearful reply was the same as she gives to Isabella, when she asks her if " she don't want to escape." That poor girl may be dead now—dissipation soon destroys its victims, but if she is—another will be hunted up by the *dealers* in the infamy of their sex, to supply her place. The death of one seems to be no warning to the others, but they continue on as before until they, too, pass away. How long shall this continue? It is left with the people of New York to say, for that they can put a stop to it, no one who possesses sense will doubt. Let them elect officers who will do their *duty*—and the city would soon present a far brighter and purer picture.

CHAPTER XVI.

THE day passed, and poor Angelina grew no better. Mr. Precise still waited by her side, and the doctor had already called several times. Her fever was at a height which made the crisis near. He knew that ere the dawn of another day her fate would be determined—the fever would turn and break; or her strength would give way entirely.

Noticing that she very often glanced at the door, and seemed to be thinking of something more than her mere illness, Mr. Precise asked:

"What do you look for, my dear? Is there anything I can do for you?"

"No, sir, thank you!" murmured the invalid. "My cousin said she'd be here before noon—I want to see her. It's strange she don't come!"

"So it is—but don't you know where she lives? I'll send for her!"

"I don't know the number, sir," replied Angelina; "it is in Thomas Street, close to Church, but she's seldom at home! You know that I told you she had led a bad life—but she wants to be good now!"

"Yes, yes! I remember. She shall have a chance to reform. I'll take care of her and her poor old father!" replied Mr. Precise.

"I've been trying to think what she meant by her strange language this morning, sir. I'm so afraid some harm is coming to you! She knows all the thieves in the city—I've heard her say, and I'm so afraid they mean to rob you or something!"

"Oh! no,—I can't think so!" replied Mr. Precise, "besides, I've very little property up here. I keep my money in bank!"

"It is very singular that she stays away so long. She seemed to love me so much—and then she had something important to tell you—but said it should be when she came again!"

"Yes,—she did seem to like you," said the old gentleman, "and she spoke so feelingly of her poor father. It made me take quite a liking to her!"

"I do so wish she'd come—there must be something wrong!" murmured the invalid.

———

There was, indeed, something wrong, and it was not by her will that Lize had broken her promise. That had been a sad day for her, so far. We will glance at some of its incidents.

She had hurried away from the lodging-house, when she found that her father was not there, and her steps were directed to the graveyard where her mother had been buried, for she remembered that her father had alluded to that spot on the evening before. For more than fifteen years she had avoided that spot—for more than fifteen years she had tried to forget that the dust of her who had brought her into the world, was there deposited.

She was not very long in reaching the place, and found upon entering it, the sexton and his assistants engaged in opening a tomb. She hurried by them without speaking, to the well remembered corner, where a broken grave-stone marked her mother's grave—but her father was not there. The ground was level—dead weeds of the last year's growth lay crushed and rotting over the spot, showing how much it had been neglected. Some mischievous urchin, or careless grave-digger, had cracked off a piece of the marble slab, destroying a portion of the simple epitaph.

"Not here!" muttered Lize, as she looked around. "Not here! Where can he be?"

Then, as she gazed upon the broken tombstone and the neglected grave, a sweeping recollection of the past came up, and her heart, brimful of grief, gave vent to its misery. She burst into a flood of tears.

"Oh, God! my mother!" she sobbed, as she bent over the spot, "how I wish that I slept down there with you!"

The neglected grave and broken monument were but too like herself. While she stood there, the hour when that grave had received its tenant came back to her memory—and, then, a still earlier one, when that fond mother had caressed and petted her, with a care and fondness which only a mother can feel. Oh! what agony was there in these remembrances to her, for they forced a contrast with her present misery!

She was aroused from her bending position, by the voice of the old sexton, who, noticing her sorrow, came to her side and said:

"You seem in trouble, Miss. Is there any grave that you can't find? I know every one in this yard—I've seen a great many of 'em filled—it's going on sixty years since I commenced here, and my father had the place before me!"

"Do you know *that* grave,—do you remember who lies there?" said Lize, looking sadly at the white-headed old man, and pointing to her mother's grave.

"Yes,—yes," replied the old man,—"her name's on my book, fees paid, and all settled. Let me see,—I remember when she was buried,—it was a rainy day, and nobody would come out of the carriages to see her put in, except the minister and one gentleman—I thought it strange; I remember—it was a dark day!"

"Yes, oh God! yes, it was a dark day!" murmured Lize; "but I've another question to ask you—did you see an old man here this morning?"

"Yes," replied the sexton; "there was one here, but he isn't here now!"

"Where did he go? did he stop here by this grave?"

Yes, my men saw him here when they came to dig the grave they're at now, but when he saw them he laughed strange-like, as if he was light-headed, and told 'em to go on and dig the grave, he'd go to get *her* ready for it. They didn't know what he meant, and when I came they told me of it!"

"Where can he have gone to now!" muttered the unhappy woman; "he must be crazy—may be he has gone back to the tavern—if so, they'll keep him till I come!"

"Was he some relation o' yours?" asked the talkative old sexton.

"He was the husband of her who is buried there, and she was my mother!" replied Lize; "I want you to clear away the weeds and raise that grave. If I live till summer, I'll plant roses upon it!"

"Yes, they grows mainly well over graves, and so does poppies! I never could account for it!" said the sexton, pocketing the piece of money which Lize handed to him. He added:

"I'll fix up the place nicely, Miss, and if you should stand in need of an undertaker before long, you can find a good one at No. 63 —— Street; he's my son-in-law, married my youngest daughter, Huldah Ann, and set up the business, 'cause, you see, I could help him a good deal. I've got another son-in-law that's a Thompsonian doctor—he married 'Lizabeth: he's a main good help to the business!"

Lize was not listening to the old sexton; she was thinking where to go in search of her father. Therefore, before he was done enumerating his sons-in-law, and their respective professions, she turned away and left him.

"I'll go to old Jack's first!" she said, "and put a stop to his robbing that good old gentleman, who is so kind to poor Angy. Then I'll stave down to the Battery as fast as I can, and see if my poor father is there! if he isn't, I'll watch by my mother's grave all night!"

Lize hurried down to old Circle's, which place she reached but a short time after Frank Hennock had left. Old Jack was delighted to see her; never before had she seen him so much pleased.

"Vont you take a drop of summat vet; I vos just thinkin' ov you!" said he.

"Well, what did you think, old stick-in-the-mud?"

"Why, my gal, I vos a thinkin' vot a huseful member of hour society you vos!"

"Then you'd hate to lose me, wouldn't you?"

"Couldn't think o' sich a thing!" replied Jack. Why there ar'n't such another panneller on the cross has can come hup to you! 'Tild' Hoag ar'n't nowhere, and the bloody houtsiders never does a job hup right! but what'll you take?"

"Nothin! come in the back room—I want to talk to ye in private!" said Lize.

"Sartin!" responded Jack; "'ere, 'Arriet, come 'ere and tend bar while I have a patter with Miss Eliza!"

The old man's daughter came in, and Circle whispered something in her ear, then led the way into the back room, where Lize alone followed him. After closing the door, he sat down, and pointing to another seat, said;

"Well, what's hup; 'ave you put your peepers on another lay?"

"No, it's not that!" said Lize; "I've come here, Jack, to get you to break up a lay that you've put up already!"

"To break up a lay, Lize? why this is su'thin' new!" said Jack, counterfeiting the utmost surprise, though Frank's information led him to expect this turn from her.

"Yes, it is," she replied; "but I've got my reasons for it!"

"Vont you say vot they is?" asked Mr. Circle.

"Yes. That man, Mr. Precise, whose crib you've given over for Black Bill and Jack Murphy to crack, has done me a favor that I'll never forget as long as I live. I want you to let him off, and to pay him back the money on that check!"

"Wot!" cried Jack in astonishment; "why wots come hover you, Lize? You ar'n't a goin' to turn a canter, are you?"

"No, I'm not going to do nothing of that sort, but I ask this of you as a favor?"

"Well, Lize, not meaning to give you a short ans'er, the lay is hall put up, and I'll be d——d if it's agoin' to be broke up!" said old Jack.

"Then, Cap'n Jack, you'll force me to put the good old man on his guard. I say he shall not be robbed!"

"So—you'd 'peach, would ye? Blow the gaff on us, as allers 'elped you out of hev'ry scrape you got hinto!"

"I don't want to blow on you, Cap'n Jack—but I've made up my mind that old man shall go free of trouble!"

"May be you'd like to be Cap'n of *the* society, eh?" said Jack sarcastically.

"No—nor what's more, I don't mean to have any more to do with you or your gang; I'll live on the square after this!"

"You will, will you! vel I've only one hobjection to that ere!"

"What is it?"

"Honly, that if you don't choose to live on the cross *with* the

the society, you shan't live on the square out of it—that's hall !"

" What do you mean, you thieving old fence !"

" I means that ve'll board you at hour own hexpense, hold gal—you needn't work for your livin !"

" I don't understand you !" said Lize.

" Don't yer ? Well, jest wait a shake, an' I'll hexplain. 'Arriet my gal, 'as the cider come yet ?"

" Two barrel, dad," replied the girl, from the bar-room.

" Have 'em fotched in, we'll stow one barrel away in the cellar !" added the old man.

As he said this, two men entered the back room. They were Black Bill and Jack Murphy, and they stepped in between the door and where Jack and Lize were seated.

" If you're agoing to have company, I'll leave !" said Lize, getting up.

" No—jist 'old hon habout a minnit !" said Jack. " I want to see wot these 'ere gentlemen 'ud say habout giving hup their lay !"

" Givin hup hour lay ?" growled Black Bill. " Wot the bloody 'ell's that fur !"

" Yis, if it's a fair questin !" added Jack Murphy, looking first at Circle and then at Lize.

" Why—that 'ere *lady*, Miss Eliza, 'as got a new kink inter her 'ead, and she wants you to give up crackin the hup-town covey's crib !"

" She be d——d !" said Bill gruffly—" let her mind her hown lays, we'll take care o' hours !"

" We'll trate the ould gintleman kindly, though, if she axes it as a favor !" said Murphy, " we'll be dacent and leave him a pair o' breeches to put on in the mornin' and a dressin gownd may be."

" I'm going !" said Lize—" I see there's no reason in you."

" Going to blow us ?" asked Jack.

" 1 didn't say that !" replied the girl.

" No—but the devil trust you, I wont, you arn't agoin' hout o' yere just yet !"

" No—I think it's rather could out o' doors, ye might take could !" said Murphy.

Black Bill didn't speak, but he put his broad shoulders against the inside of the door and folded his arms with an air of quiet determination.

"So—you'll keep me a prisoner?" asked Lize.

"Not meanin' for to give you a short answer, I'm d——d if we don't," replied Jack.

"What, if I promise not to peach!"

"You'd forget your promise, may be, as easy as you make it!"

"No—no, you must let me out, I want to go and look for my father!" said Lize, who began to be a little frightened at the prospect before her. "I was only joking with you, Jack, I wouldn't blow the gaff for nothing!"

"An' a pleasant joke it was," cried Murphy, "an' it's only a joke Cap'n Jack is a playin' on ye, now!"

"Come—come, let me go," pleaded Lize—"I'll not tell, I must go to see my father and my cousin!"

"Och, and hav'n't ye niver an uncle too, that ye want to be lookin' afther?" said Murphy, who seemed much to enjoy the poor girl's trouble.

"There's no use o' humbuggin', Jack!" growled Black Bill, "she's on the trap—let her slide!"

Just at that moment, Jack, who had 'risen and passed over to the side of the room, touched a ring that appeared to be fastened to the ceiling, and Lize felt herself suddenly sinking—the floor seeming to yield beneath her weight. She made a spring towards the door—but was thrust back by Murphy, and in another moment she was hidden in darkness below—the trap having canted and left her upon the ground, in a deep cellar below the room where she had been seated. In a moment, the trap was back in the same place as before, and only the stifled shrieks of poor Lize could be heard.

"Well, that's what I call a rum go!" said Black Bill, after the trap had closed.

"Better come out an' take a go o' rum, to settle your stummac!" said old Jack, coolly. "She'll be heasy enough, 'till 'arter you've cracked the old 'un's crib! I'll tend to her!"

"A very sinsible remark o' yours!" said Murphy, "an' one, I think, as 'll raise no 'jections on our part. By the way, Cap'n Jack, a matthew-matty-call questi'n 'as jist revolved itself inter my craminyum!"

" Vel, vot is it ?" asked old Jack.

" Why, I've often heard, 'mongst *orthers*, an' other unfort'nate individuals, this 'ere question revolved : whether it wer' possible to square a circle ? What's your opinion—as the devil asked of the minister, when he quoted scriptur' to him !"

" Why, don't know as I see the sense o' the thing," replied Jack ;—" if it means that one o' the Circle family ever was known to cruise on the square—it's a bloody lie. The whole breed was born on the cross, an' they'll live on it, that's as sure as mad dogs in July !"

" Then it's yer opinion that the Circle can't be squared ?"

" Hexactly !" replied old Jack.

" Thin I'll be afther takin' a drink wid ye, for I'm of the same persuasion, as the divil said to the Methodist !" replied Murphy.

The party now adjourned to the bar-room.

CHAPTER XVII.

CHARLES MEADOWS came down to his mother's breakfast-table, pale and haggard, on the morning after his midnight interview with Carlton. He noticed, also, that his mother looked weary and unwell, as if she, like him, had passed a sleepless night; but she, with a mother's anxiety, was the first to speak.

"Poor Charles! You're sick this morning!" she exclaimed. "Mr. S—— must not keep you up so late!"

"It is nothing, mother!" said he with a forced smile, "we are very busy down at the store, and since he has raised my salary, I must do all I can, you know, for his interest!"

"Yes, that's true, but still you musn't hurt your health, or you will not long have the strength to earn your salary!"

"Oh! never fear, mother, I shall keep my strength as long as I need it—but you look unwell, mother—what is the matter with you?"

"I slept very badly, my son, and I had such a horrible dream about you and your sister!"

"A dream about us—what was it, mother?"

"I hate to think of it," replied the old lady, with a shudder—"it was dreadful;—but I do wish you'd go and see 'Bella, I'm afraid she's sick!"

"No danger of that, mother,—I saw Harry Whitmore just as I was coming home last night, and he said he'd just left her and his sister, well and hearty!"

"But wont you go and see her this morning?" urged the mother.

"I'll not have time to-day, mother—but it's likely she'll come home during the day—if she don't, I'll go and see her this evening, if I can possibly spare the time!"

"Well, do—I cannot drive that terrible dream from my mind!"

" What was it, mother? do tell me!"

" Why, it was this, my son. I thought I saw your sister walking through a very beautiful meadow, gathering flowers which grew very thickly along the banks of a little brook, and I was with her. Suddenly she saw a very handsome flower, on the other side of the brook, and though it was too wide for her to cross easily, she went back, and took a running start and leaped over it. She laughed, and called to me to come over, but I could not.

" Then she ran on, and bent down to pick up the flower from its stem, when she started back with a scream, and cried to me that a bee had stung her.

" I called to her to return to me,—but she said she could not —that she was very weak and faint.

" Then she came and sat down upon the opposite bank of the stream, and I saw that she was very pale, and I told her to dip her hands in the water and bathe her forehead.

" She put her hand to the stream to do so, but drew it back quickly, and cried out that it was hot, that it burned her. I was very much frightened then, and determined to cross over and help her—but the stream suddenly commenced boiling and hissing, and I saw that it was full of horrible snakes, that were crawling about on its bottom, some of them biting each other. They were all kinds and colors, some of them pretty, with all the hues of the rainbow; others, black and slimy! Oh! it was a terrible sight!"

The old lady paused and hid her eyes with her hands, as if to shut out the vision—and shuddered.

" Go on, mother—go on!" said Charles, interested in this singular dream.

" Well, I screamed to 'Bella to run back from the snakes. She looked over into the water, and laughed, and said she didn't see any snakes, and just at that moment, I saw one of the largest—a golden-hued and bright-skinned serpent, move slowly towards her.

" She didn't see it, and when I screamed to her to run away, looked mournfully at me and said :

" 'You must be going crazy, mother !'

" I screamed and screamed to her—for the snake was crawling up all this time, and was now on the bank close to her, bu·

she d.dn't seem to see, till at last it was at her feet.   Then she laughed, and called to me :

"'See here, mother, what a sweet pretty dove this is !' and she took its head in her hands and kissed it.

"Oh, mercy ! What a horrible sight it was. I screamed to her—but she looked sadly at me, and said :

"'Poor mother, I'm sorry you're crazy. It wasn't my fault !'

"And then she took the snake up in her arms, and it began to grow larger and larger until it was as large as a man almost, and then she seemed to know what it was, for she screamed and prayed to me for help.

"But I could not move—it seemed as if I had grown to the ground like a tree, and I could not even speak.

"Oh God, it was horrible ! The snake kept folding around and around her form in great slimy folds—and her face grew dark—and her eyes turned red with agony, and her tongue stuck out from her mouth, and the blood streamed down from bursting veins upon her bosom, and yet I could not help her.

"Then I saw the head of the snake and it had a human face—a face just like Mr. Whitmore's. Oh! I'm so afraid some harm 'll come to the poor girl through him !"

"P'shaw, mother—it was only a dream !" replied the son—"Harry Whitmore is the very soul of honor. I would trust him quicker than any man in town. Besides, he loves Bella—has openly told me so, and as I know only waits to get his mother's consent to offer her his hand in honorable marriage !"

"Well, well—we are all in the hands of God !" murmured the mother.

"But go on—tell me all your dream !"

"Well"—continued the old lady—"I looked at poor Bella, till I saw her a crushed, blackened, and shapeless mass, and then it seemed as if wings were given to me to fly away from the dreadful spot, and I found myself in a town. It seemed to be night, but I could see as plainly as if it was broad day-light. I saw you—and I was trying to get to you to tell you about poor 'Bella, when you looked at me and motioned to me to keep back. I couldn't think what you meant, but I saw you step into a little shadow and crouch down as if you wanted to hide yourself. And then I noticed you had a pistol in your hand !"

"A pistol, mother!" shrieked the young man, springing from his seat, and turning pale.

"Yes, child; but what is the matter?"

"Nothing, mother, nothing! go on, it is *only* a dream!"

She continued:

"I tried to go to you, but again it seemed as if I was fastened to the earth. Then I saw a man and a woman walking along towards where you were. The woman was very pale, and was weeping; but she didn't look like our 'Bella!"

"Go on, mother! go on, tell me all!" cried the son, impatiently.

"Well, they two came on till they got just where you were, and there they stopped, and the woman went on talking to the man, and crying. But he seemed stern and cold, and then she acted as if she were pleading to him for some favor.

"But he shook his head, and pushed her back from him, when she tried to kiss him.

"Then she seemed to get angry, and shook her clenched hand at him and stamped her foot upon the ground, and just then you crept slowly out from the shade and——"

"*Killed* him! say, mother, did I kill him?" screamed Meadows, interrupting his mother, and glaring upon her with eyes that seemed to be bursting from their sockets.

"Oh mercy! my son! what is the matter?" shrieked the old lady; "don't be so excited, it was only a dream!"

"True, mother, true, but I was so excited in it, that I had forgotten myself. Pray, go on; I will not interrupt you again!"

"Well," she continued, "I watched you steal out carefully behind him, until you got so close that you could touch him; and the woman saw you, too, but didn't say anything, till you raised your hand with the pistol in it close to his head; and then she turned and ran away. Just at the same moment, I saw the smoke, and heard a noise, as if your pistol had gone off, and I screamed and woke up!"

"Oh horrible—horrible!" groaned the son, while great drops of sweat came out upon his brow, and then he murmured:

"It is *only* a dream!"

"Yes, child, that's all. Don't take on about it, or I shall be sorry I told you!"

"Don't you believe dreams come true sometimes, mother?" asked the son.

"Well, I don't know. They used to in the bible days, but I hope these wont!" she replied—"I know they can't! 'Bella is as pure as a snow-drop, and I know you're too good to kill a man; when you were a boy, you wouldn't so much as kill a fly, like the other boys!"

"Wouldn't I?" asked the young man, in a thoughtful manner.

"No—nor even fight with your schoolmates, except they forced a fight on you!"

"Then you think I'd not have spunk enough to kill a man!" said the clerk with a strange, wild laugh.

"I hope you'd never have the heart to do it!" replied Mrs. Meadows.

"Not even in self-defence, eh?" continued Charles.

"Why, I suppose that *would* be different!" replied the old lady—"but I hope you'll never be placed in such a dreadful necessity!"

The young man shuddered, but did not reply.

"Why don't you eat your breakfast—it's all getting cold. I do declare you haven't eaten a mouthful!" cried the mother.

"Your dreams have spoiled my appetite!" replied he.

"Oh, never mind them, my son—they're *only* dreams. I s'pose I was thinking of you and 'Bella, when I went to sleep—come, drink your coffee!"

"No—I cannot! It is time I went down to the store," replied the son. "I don't feel very well this morning!"

"Poor child, you *do* look sick! You must have more sleep—there's nothing wears young folks out more quickly than want of rest and irregular hours!"

"But I must attend to business, mother!"

"Not at the expense of your health, my dear son. I'd rather live on less than to see you look so pale and care-worn."

"You're a good, kind mother!" said the son feelingly. "We'll all do well, and be happy bye and bye!"

"I hope so," sighed the mother—"we've seen pretty close times—but yet we have no right to complain, for there are those in this great city who'd be very glad to change situations with us !"

"Not with me !" thought the unhappy clerk—"not with me, surrounded as I am by everything to make me wretched."

Those fearful dreams had thrown a cloud over his heart, and he could neither eat nor smile. He soon started down towards his store. While on his way, he met Gus. Livingston, who was just leaving his hotel, to fulfil the errand of Whitmore at Madame Swett's.

"Good morning, Charley," said the young man. "Why you look as if you'd been washed out in dirty water, and not ironed yet ! What's the matter with you ?"

"I was up rather late, and drank some of that infernal brandy at Carlton's. I do believe that they drug their sideboard liquor at every gambling house in town !"

"Well, I've heard it said—but I don't believe it !" replied Gus., "but have you heard about poor Harry Whitmore ?"

"No—what is the matter ? is he in trouble ?" asked the clerk.

"Why, he nearly got his brains knocked out last night, and his right arm is broken !"

"You don't say so ! How was it ?"

"Why, he was a little in for it, I think—you know he drank considerable of Carlton's brandy, and he seemed to be in a fighting humor, and he soon got accommodated. He met a crowd of the Bowery Boys, and they administered particular goss to him, hit him over the head and broke his arm with a slungshot, or some such musical instrument !"

"Poor fellow ! Where is he ?"

"Up stairs, in my room—but he's got lots of company. Jim Decatur, Count Lijah, and two or three more are having a quiet game of poker—and Harry is betting away on their hands, just to pass off the time. He was a little cross about it at first, but nothing puts him out, and he takes it as easy as a navy parson takes a fight !"

"I'll try and see him to-night.—Does his sister know of it ?" asked Charles.

"No—and by the way, he begged not to let it be known to them. If I was you I'd keep close, or else not see her at all—

at any rate wait till he gets better.   We've all promised to keep still—but I thought I'd better tell you!"

"Yes—thank you, I'm glad you did—for I think a great deal of Harry!"

"Yes—yes, you've reason to!" laughed Gus., "he thinks so much of you and your family.   By the way, isn't he a little attentive to Miss Isabella?"

"That is best known to him and her!" said Meadows, carelessly.   "I never pry into my sister's secrets!"

"Well, that's the best way!" said Gus., laughing, "I see you're going down town.   I'm going down a little ways, I'll walk with you!"

"Certainly—I shall be glad of your company!" said the clerk.

"I wonder what's become of Mary—the cigar girl?" said Gus., as they passed the store where she usually was seen.

"I don't know, is she not at the same place?" asked Charles.

"No—she hasn't been there for some days!" replied the other. "I've heard rumors about her going off with an English lord, but I don't believe them.   I asked Sam Selden, but he only grinned and showed his white teeth, and said he didn't know.   She is an almighty pretty girl, though, isn't she!"

"I've never noticed her particularly!" replied Meadows.

"Yes, I know you're rather offish when the fair sex are in the way," said Gus.   "You're like me, a devilish sight too modest."

"Isn't that Henry Carlton coming up the street?" asked Meadows.

"Yes—I believe it is, and there's Sam Selden with him. They hunt in couples—rather a strange way, too, for bloodhounds!"

"Let's go in somewhere, I want to avoid him!" said Charles, turning pale.

"Well—let's go up into Ma'am P.'s, here at the corner!" replied the young man.   "She keeps various kinds of refreshments in her place, and you can get anything you want from a gin cocktail, up!"

"Anywhere—to avoid him!" said the clerk—"I've reasons for not wishing to see him this morning!"

"Well, we'll go up into Madame P.'s, and see how she is this morning. Carlton won't come up there, for he don't like her over and above middling, I've heard—though I can't tell why. Her trade oughtn't to hurt his any !"

The two turned down a narrow street which leads out of Broadway, and were about entering a door which opened on their right, when Meadows heard himself called by name.

He turned and saw that Carlton was approaching.

"I wish to see you a minute, Meadows," said he in a familiar tone—"just an instant !"

"Come in and take a drink with us !" said Gus., before Meadows had time to answer.

"No, sir, I don't patronize such establishments as that !" said Carlton sternly ; then altering his tone, he added :

"I'll not detain you a moment, Meadows, I have some little arrangement to speak of in regard to that contract !"

"Well, sir—I'll hear you !" replied the clerk, gloomily.

"I'll go up stairs then, and wait for you !" said Gus—"shall I call for anything and have it mixed for you ?"

"Just ask Madame P. the price of linen this morning, for me," said Sam Selden, showing his white teeth.

"I will !" said Gus—"Can I do anything more for you ?"

"No—not this morning, thank you—but as I see you've your white kid gloves on this morning, let me recommend you a practice of my own invention—one which combines economy, cleanliness, and comfort !" replied the handsome gambler.

"What is it ?" said Gus, "I know you're a man of taste !"

"Why, always call for a *tube* when you drink ale. It saves the glove and prevents the foam from touching one's moustache !"

"That's a devilish good idea !"

"Certainly—I mean to take out a patent for it !" replied Sam, with a smile.

Livingston saw that Meadows was still engaged in conversation with Carlton, and went up stairs to pay his respects to the lady who kept the various kinds of refreshments.

"Good morning, madam !" said he, as he entered a small saloon in the second story.

He addressed a rather florid lady, who looked decidedly English, and with one exception, might have answered for one of the beauties which George IV. designated as " fat, fair, and forty." What that exception was, we will not be so ungallant as to say.

The lady smiled, as she received the salutation of her visitor, and said:

"How *do* you do, Mr. Livingston? I haven't seen you, I don't know when! Why you look as fresh as a rose this morning!"

"Thank you, ma'am, I need not say that you look like a morning-glory,—but I had a question for you, which a gentleman requested me to ask just now!"

"Indeed! what was it?" asked the lady.

"Why, Sam Selden; you know Sam, don't you?"

"Yes, I guess I do, the bloody scapegallows; I wonder if he didn't have somethin' to do with the takin' away of my gas fixtures! But what did he have to say?" replied the landlady, turning redder than usual, if possible.

"Why, he told me to ask you the price of linen!"

"He did, did he! just ask him the price o' hemp when you see him, and tell him I don't mind spendin' a sixpence whenever he wants a couple o' fathoms o' rope!" cried Mrs. P., who seemed strangely enraged at the question propounded by Livingston.

"You and Sam don't seem to hitch together!" said Gus.

"No, nor we never would, if we lived together a thousand years, and there was only us two in the world!" replied the old woman. "There are some gamblers as *is* men, and them I like well enough; but for *him*, he's the smallest kind of a very small breed o' potatoes, in my opinion!"

"Well, we'll not quarrel about him!" replied Gus, "but I'm thirsty!"

"That seems to be a prevailin' complaint amongst my visitors!" replied Madame P. "What'll it be, Mr. Livingston? I've a first rate stock of refreshments on hand!"

"Especially dry goods!" said Gus., with a laugh.

"There it is again!" cried the landlady. "That Sam Selden has been a talkin' to you, I know—but it's too hard if a body can't do a quiet legitimate business without being talked about. It's all along o' my being a poor widder woman, with no man for a protector—but never mind, my time 'll come by and by. What 'll you have, Mr. Livingston?"

"Why, I've heard, too, that you understand the proportioning of gin cocktails very well!" said Gus.

"Shouldn't wonder if I did!" replied Madame P. "I've made many a one in my day!"

"Then have the kindness to make one for me!" said Gus., "and by the way, mix two. I've a young friend that'll be up here in a moment, one Charley Meadows; he's rather green!"

"Is he flush—will he stand bleeding?" asked the lady.

"Well, don't know—he's rather green—he might be led to examine into the dry goods line!" replied Gus. with a wink.

We regret, dear reader, that we must defer the remainder of this scene until the next number—but you will not have long to wait.

END OF PART FOUR.

www.ingramcontent.com/pod-product-compliance
Lightning Source LLC
LaVergne TN
LVHW081346060426
835508LV00017B/1445